FAMILIES AND AGING

LINDA BURTON
Editor

GENERATIONS AND AGING SERIES

Originally published as the Summer 1992 issue of GENERATIONS, Journal of the American Society on Aging, Mary Johnson, Editor.

Baywood Publishing Company, Inc.
Amityville, New York

Library of Congress Catalog Number: 92-42277
ISBN: 0-89503-114-0

Library of Congress Cataloging-in-Publication Data

Families and aging / Linda Burton, editor.
    p.   cm. – – (Generations and aging series)
  "Originally published as the Summer 1992 issue of Generations,
Journal of the American Society on Aging."
  Includes bibliographical references.
  ISBN 0-89503-114-0
  1. Aged– –United States– –Social conditions. 2. Aged– –United
States– –Family relationships.   3. Minority aged– –United States–
–Family relationships.   I. Burton, Linda.   II. Generations (San
Francisco, Calif.)   III. Series.
HQ1064.U5F278 1992
305.26'0973—dc20   92-42277
                                            CIP

Table of Contents

Chapter 1

Introduction:
Families and the Aged:
Issues of Complexity and Diversity

Linda Burton

The family lives of older Americans are no longer as simple or as homogeneous as some historical accounts suggest (Elder, 1981; Hareven, 1978). Three interrelated phenomena, all of which have occurred in the last century, are transforming traditional perceptions and expectations concerning families and the elderly in contemporary American society. The first and most familiar is the "demographic revolution" (Uhlenberg, 1978; Wells, 1982; Watkins, Menken and Bongaarts, 1987). Characterized by declines in mortality and fertility and a rise in divorce, the demographic revolution has "changed the complexion of family life" (Hagestad, 1988, p. 405). Individuals are now more likely to grow older in four- or even five-generation families, spend an unprecedented number of years in family roles such as grandparenthood, and be part of a more complex and varied web of intergenerational family ties (Bengtson, Rosenthal and Burton, 1990; Hagestad, 1986; Riley, 1983).

The second phenomenon affecting the family lives of the elderly concerns the dramatic increase in cultural, ethnic, and racial diversity in the American population. Through processes such as immigration and integration, and choices concerning nontraditional lifestyles, the American population represents a "potpourri" of family "lifeways"

(Gelfand, 1989; Taeuber, 1990). These lifeways reflect the legacies of Asian, African American, Hispanic, Native American, and European cultural norms and beliefs about family, and the creation of alternative family arrangements by single parents, gay men and lesbians, and others. This diversity in family lifeways coupled with demographic transitions translate into a complex mosaic of family structures, processes, roles, and relationships for aging individuals.

In addition, the family lives of the aged are shaped by a third phenomenon—the social and economic condition of American society. For example, economic setbacks experienced in some families because of a troubled national economy prompt families to develop a variety of adaptive strategies to survive (Elder, 1974). While some families can rely on generating internal economic resources within the extended kin network to meet their needs, other families may be so economically pressed that they look to external sources, such as community social services, for help (Johnson and Barer, 1990; Stack and Burton, in press). The range of strategies developed by families to address social and economic challenges is thus another layer in the mosaic that is family life for aged Americans.

The purpose of this volume is to highlight the complexity and diversity of issues concerning contemporary families and the elderly. The topics covered are of course not an exhaustive treatment of this field of study; they do, however, address a broad array of scholarly, practical, and policy-related interests concerning contemporary family structures, processes, roles, and relationships as they affect and are affected by the lives of older Americans.

To begin, the complexity and diversity of contemporary families and the elderly can best be understood when discussed in the context of historical time. Tamara Hareven opens this volume with a comprehensive overview of the evolution of kin relationships and the elderly in America from the nineteenth century to current times. Given historical transformations in the structure and function of families, Hareven suggests that there have been major changes in the attitudes and the ability of families to provide assistance to older relatives. Hareven argues that these historical changes teach us a lesson—that in order for the needs of the current elderly population to be met, families and social services will have to jointly provide necessary support.

Complementing the work of Hareven, Christine Himes provides an insightful discussion of the effects of the "demographic revolution" on the family lives of older Hispanic, white, and African Americans. She notes that given declines in mortality and fertility, future generations of older people may be part of more "top-heavy" vertical family structures. These vertical intergenerational family connections, however, may become quite complicated as older individuals become members of "blended" multigenerational families, a product of divorce and remarriage among their adult children.

In the chapter, "Divorced and Reconstituted Families," Colleen Johnson explores the impact of marital dissolution and remarriage on the lives of older generations in families. Citing evidence from a longitudinal study of suburban families in which marital changes had recently occurred, Johnson describes the diversity of experiences grandparents have with their grandchildren when their adult children divorce and remarry.

An undergirding theme in this volume concerns ethnic and racial variability in the family lives of the elderly. Consistent with the theme of ethnic/racial diversity, Barbara Yee profiles the intergenerational family issues of an emerging group of older Americans—Southeast Asian refugees. Doreen Der-McLeod and Jennie Chin Hansen provide a description of On Lok Senior Health Services of San Francisco—a multiethnic comprehensive support program for aged individuals and their families. Peggye Dilworth-Anderson explores the past and future of extended family supports for older African Americans. Carla Walls considers the role of black churches as an alternative form of "family support" for African American elderly. And David Eggebeen examines racial and other variables in intergenerational exchanges between the elderly and their adult children.

A recurrent family role addressed in a number of chapters is grandparenthood. Current research on grandparenthood indicates that the role is more tenuous and diverse in contemporary society than historically-based images of grandmothers and grandfathers suggest (Barranti, 1985; Bengtson and Robertson, 1985; Kivett, 1991; Cherlin and Furstenberg, 1986; Presser, 1989). For example, there is tremendous variability in the amount of involvement grandparents have with their grandchildren (Troll, 1983; Burton and Bengtson, 1985; Hagestad and Burton, 1986). Some grandparents assume the role of surrogate parent to their grandchildren, while others remain relatively uninvolved. Within the context of variable involvement with their grandchildren, grandparents experience challenges as well as opportunities to contribute to the family development. Linda Burton and Cynthia deVries describe some of the challenges and opportunities voiced by 101 African American grandparents who participated in their qualitative studies of intergenerational family processes.

The emerging changes in the family lives of older Americans have not only drawn attention to the traditional family structures, processes, relationships, and roles, but also to topics rarely studied in the field. This issue highlights several of these topics. For example, Douglas Kimmel discusses family issues for older gay men and lesbians. Lori McElhaney provides an overview of the existing literature on dating among elderly Americans. Martha Moyer offers insights on a familial relationship that is becoming of increasing importance to the aged—the relationship between elderly siblings. Bonnie Genevay explores the issues faced by the elderly who live alone. And Lillian Troll and Vern Bengston examine the family relationships of the fastest growing subpopulation of the aged—the oldest-old.

This volume concludes with a focus on policy and programs for families and the elderly. Greta Winbush challenges us to examine the "conceptual" basis on which we design and administer social support to those who provide care for elderly family members. Majorie Cantor describes the necessary linkages that must occur between social services, community supports, and families to meet the growing needs of elderly Americans. Ute Bayen provides a guide to further readings in this area.

It is my hope that readers of this volume come away with heightened interest in exploring the complexity and diversity of families and aging. Clearly, this complexity and diversity will generate new research, policy, and program agendas that address emerging issues and needs for elderly Americans and their families. This volume is an effort toward that end—an effort toward fostering a "new look" at families and aging.

REFERENCES

Barranti, C. C. R., 1985. "The Grandparent/Grandchild Relationship: Family Resources in an Era of Voluntary Bonds." *Family Relations* 34:343–52.

Bengtson, V. L., Rosenthal, C. and Burton, L., 1990. "Families and Aging: Diversity and Heterogeneity." In R. Binstock and L. George, Handbook of Aging and Social Sciences. New York: Academic Press.

Bengtson, V. L. and Robertson, J. F., eds., 1985. *Grandparenthood: Research and Policy Perspectives*. Beverly Hills, Calif.: Sage.

Burton, L. M. and Bengtson, V. L., 1985. "Black Grandmothers: Issues of Timing and Meaning in Roles." In V. L. Bengtson and J. F. Robertson, eds., *Grandparenthood: Research and Policy Perspectives*. Beverly Hills, Calif.: Sage.

Cherlin, A. J. and Furstenberg, F. F., 1986. *The New American Grandparent: A Place in the Family, A Life Apart*. New York: Basic Books.

Elder, G. H., Jr., 1974. *Children of the Great Depression: Social Change in Life Experience*. Chicago: University of Chicago Press.

Elder, G. H., Jr., 1981. "History and the Family: The Discovery of Complexity." *Journal of Marriage and the Family* 43(3): 489–519.

Gelfand, D., 1989. "Immigration, Aging, and Intergenerational Relationships." *Gerontologist* 29:366–72.

Hagestad, G. O., 1986. "The Aging Society as a Context for Family Life." *Daedalus* 115:119–39.

Hagestad, G. O., 1988. "Demographic Change and the Life Course: Some Emerging Trends in the Family Realm." *Family Relations* 37:405–10.

Hagestad, G. O. and Burton, L. M., 1986. "Grandparenthood, Life Context, and Family Development." *American Behavioral Scientist* 29:471–84.

Hareven, T. K., ed., 1978. *Transitions: The Family and the Life Course in Historical Perspective*. New York: Academic Press.

Johnson, C. L. and Barer, B. M., 1990. "Families and Networks among Older Inner-City Blacks." *Gerontologist* 30(6): 726–33.

Kivett, V. R., 1991. "The Grandparent-Grandchild Connection." *Marriage and Family Review* 16(3/4):267–90.

Presser, H. B., 1989. "Some Economic Complexities of Child Care Provided by Grandmothers." *Journal of Marriage and the Family* 51:581–91.

Riley, M. W., 1983. "The Family in an Aging Society: A Matrix of Latent Relationships." *Journal of Family Issues* 4:439–54.

Stack, C. B. and Burton, L. M., in press. "Kinscripts." *Journal of Comparative Family Studies*.

Taeuber, C., 1990. "Diversity: The Dramatic Reality." In S.A. Bass, E. A. Kutza, F. M. Torres-Gil, eds., *Diversity in Aging*. Glenview, Ill.: Scott, Foresman.

Troll, L., 1983. "Grandparents: The Family Watchdogs." In T. Brubaker, ed., *Family Relationships in Later Life*. Beverly Hills, Calif.: Sage.

Ulhenberg, P., 1978. "Changing Configurations of the Life Course." In T. Hareven, ed., *Transitions: The Family and the Life Course in Historical Perspective*. New York: Academic Press.

Watkins, S. C., Menken, J. A. and Bongaarts, J., 1987. "Demographic Foundations of Family Change." *American Sociological Review* 52:346–58.

Wells, R. V., 1982. *Revolutions in Americans' Lives*. Westport, Conn.: Greenwood Press.

Chapter 2

Family and Generational Relations in the Later Years: A Historical Perspective

Tamara K. Hareven

An understanding of the family arrangements and supports for older people in American society has been clouded by myths about the past, on the one hand, and by a narrow treatment of contemporary problems, on the other hand. A historical perspective is needed, not only to understand what changes have occurred over time, but also to determine how historical events and circumstances have affected each cohort in terms of the "historical baggage" that different groups bring into old age. A life course perspective is needed in order to understand the impact of historical conditions on the life history of various cohorts and the consequences of those conditions for adaptation in the later years of life.[1]

Following a historical and life course perspective, this chapter examines changes in demographic behavior, in family and household organization, in the timing of life course transitions, and in kin assistance of men and women as these factors affected their adaptation in the later years of life in American society since the nineteenth century.

---

[1] A cohort is an age group sharing a common historical experience.

7

MYTHS ABOUT THE PAST

Historical research has dispelled the myths about the existence of ideal three-generational families in the American past: There never was an era when coresidence of three generations in the same household was the dominant familial arrangement. The "great extended families" that became part of the folklore of modern industrial society were rarely in existence. Like families today, families in the past tended to reside in nuclear units. Early American households and families were simple in their structure and did not contain extended kin. The older generation was residing in households separate from those of their children. Given the high mortality rate, most grandparents could not have expected to overlap with their grandchildren over a significant period of their lives. It would thus be futile to argue that industrialization destroyed the great extended family of the past. In reality, such a family type rarely existed.

Nor was there a "golden age" in the family relations of older people in the American or European past. Even in the Colonial period, the aged were insecure in their familial supports, though they were more revered and accorded higher social status than today. The very fact that aging parents had to enter into contracts with their inheriting sons in order to secure supports in old age in exchange for land, suggests the potential tensions and insecurities in such arrangements (Demos, 1978; Greven, 1970; Smith, 1973). Similarly, older people were not guaranteed supports from their children in urban industrial society in the nineteenth and early twentieth centuries. Familial supports and care for older people, as well as all other types of kin assistance, have always been voluntary, based on reciprocal relations over the life course. Kin were engaged, however, in more intensive relations of mutual assistance than today.

The rejection of the myth of the extended multigenerational family should not be misconstrued to mean that old people lived in isolation. Solitary residence was most uncommon throughout the nineteenth century for all age groups. The characteristic form of residence has been one where the older generation maintained separate households from those of their married children. Autonomy in old age, partly expressed in the opportunity for older people to head their own households, hinged on some form of support from an adult child living at home or on the presence of unrelated individuals in the household. The ideal was one of proximity in residence on the same land in rural areas, or in the same building or same neighborhood in urban areas. "Intimacy from a distance," the preferred mode of generational relations in contemporary American society, has been persistent since the early settlement and reaches back into the European past.

A HISTORICAL LIFE-COURSE PERSPECTIVE

The emergence of old age as a social problem can be best understood in the context of the entire life course and of the historical changes affecting people in various stages of life. In the same way, an understanding of the current problems of the family relations of older people and their supports in contemporary American society depends on a knowledge of the larger processes of change that have affected the timing of life course transitions and family and generational relations.

The adaptation of individuals and their families to the social and economic conditions they face in the later years of life is contingent on the pathways by which they reach old age (Hareven, 1981). These affect their views of family relations, their expectations of support from kin, and their ability to interact with welfare agencies and institutions. Following a historical life-course perspective, one does not view older people simply as a homogeneous group, but rather as age cohorts moving through history, each cohort with its distinct life experiences, which were shaped by the historical circumstances it encountered earlier in life (Elder, 1978). A life course perspective enables us to interpret individual and family life transitions as part of a continuous process of historical change.

DEMOGRAPHIC CHANGE

Demographic changes in American society since the late nineteenth century have significantly affected age configuration within the family and the timing of life course transitions and have had, therefore, a significant impact on the later years of life (Uhlenberg, 1974, 1978; Hareven, 1976). The decline in mortality has resulted in greater uniformity in the life course of American families and has dramatically increased the opportunities for intact survival of the family unit over the lifetime of its members (Uhlenberg, 1974, 1978). The chances for children to survive to adulthood and to grow up with their siblings and both parents alive have increased over time.

Similarly, the chances for women to fulfill the societal script of their family lives have increased dramatically. The culturally established life-course sequence for women—marriage, motherhood, survival with a husband through parenting, the launching of children, and widowhood—was experienced in the nineteenth century by only 44 percent of females born in 1870 who survived beyond age 15. The remaining 56 percent never achieved this "normal" life-course pattern, because they died young, never married, or were childless, or because their marriage was broken by the death of their husbands. As one moves into the twentieth century, an increasing portion of the population has lived out its life in family units, except when disrupted by divorce (Uhlenberg, 1974).

Under the impact of demographic, economic, and cultural factors, the timing of such transitions as leaving home, entry into and exit from the labor force, marriage, parenthood, the "empty nest," and widowhood has changed considerably over the past century. In the twentieth century, transitions to adulthood have become more uniform for the age cohort undergoing them, more orderly in sequence, and more rapidly timed. Timing has become more regulated according to specific age norms, rather than in relation to the needs of the family. Individual life transitions have become less closely synchronized with collective family ones, thus causing a further separation between the generations.

The nineteenth century pattern of transitions, which occurred more gradually and were timed less rigidly (Modell, Furstenberg and Hershberg, 1976), allowed for a wider age spread within the family and for greater opportunity for interaction among parents and adult children. Demographic changes, combined with the increasing rapidity in the timing of the transitions to adulthood, more geographic separation between an individual's family of origin and family of procreation, and the introduction of publicly regulated transitions, such as mandatory retirement, have converged to isolate and segregate age groups in the larger society. These changes have generated new kinds of stresses on familial needs and obligations.

FAMILY TRANSITIONS INTO OLD AGE

In the nineteenth century, transitions to the "Empty nest," to widowhood, and out of household headship followed no ordered sequence and extended over a relatively longer time period. Older women did experience more marked transitions than did men, although the continuing presence of adult children in the household meant that widowhood did not necessarily represent a dramatic transition into solitary residence (Chudacoff and Hareven, 1979; Hareven, 1981; Smith, 1979).

The most marked discontinuity in the life course has been the "empty nest" in a couple's middle age. The twentieth century combination of earlier marriage and fewer children overall, with segregation of childbearing to the early stages of the family cycle and children's leaving home more uniformly earlier in their parents' lives, has resulted in a more widespread emergence of the empty nest as a characteristic of the middle and later years of life (Glick, 1977).[2] At the same time, women's tendency to live longer than men has resulted in a protracted period of widowhood in the later years. These changes have led to a separation between the generations when parents are still in middle age and to a longer period for aged couples or widowed mothers without children in the household.

By contrast, in the nineteenth century, later age at marriage, higher fertility, and shorter life expectancy rendered different family configurations. The parenting period, with children remaining in the household, extended over a longer time, sometimes over the parents' entire life. Most important, the nest was rarely empty, because usually one adult child was expected to remain at home while the parents were aging (Hareven, 1976, 1982).

Aging parents strove to maintain their autonomy by retaining the headship of their own households, rather than move in with relatives or with strangers. This powerful commitment to the continued autonomy of the household was clearly in conflict with the needs of people as they were aging. In the absence of adequate public and institutional supports, older people striving to maintain independent households were caught in the double bind of living separately from their children yet having to rely on their children's assistance in order to do so.

Aging parents who were unable to live alone were either joined by an adult child, who returned to live with them, or moved into a child's household. Elderly couples who had no children, or whose children had left home, took in boarders and lodgers as part of a special exchange arrangement. Boarding provided an important means

---

[2]Over the past decade, the empty nest has begun to fill up again with young adult children who return to the parental home, or with those who never left.

of mutual exchanges between the generations even if they were not related. About one-third of the men and women in their twenties and thirties in nineteenth century American urban communities boarded with other families. For young men and women in a transitional stage between their departure from their parents' homes and the establishment of their own families, boarding offered surrogate familial settings. For older people, particularly for widows, it provided the extra income needed to maintain their own residence. It also helped to avert loneliness after the children had left home (Modell and Hareven, 1973). In some cases the function was reversed, and older people who could not live alone, but who had no children or relatives, boarded in other people's households. Solitary residence, a practice that has become increasingly prominent among older people today, was rarely experienced in the nineteenth century (Kobrin, 1976).

FAMILY STRATEGIES

The family was the most critical agent in initiating and managing life transitions. The timing of individual members' life transitions was a critical factor in the family's efforts to maintain control over its resources, especially by balancing different members' contributions to the family economy. In modern society, we are accustomed to thinking of most transitions to family roles and work careers as individual. In the past, individual members' transitions had to be synchronized with family needs and obligations. Early life transitions were bound up with later ones in a continuum of familial need and obligations. Leaving home, getting married, or setting up a separate household had to be timed in relation to one's family of origin, especially in consideration of the needs of parents as they were aging.

Under the historical conditions in which familial assistance was the almost exclusive source of security, the multiplicity of obligations that individuals incurred over life toward their relatives was more complex than in contemporary society. In addition to the ties they retained with their family of origin, individuals carried obligations toward their families of procreation and toward their spouses' family of origin. Such obligations cast individuals into various overlapping and, at times, conflicting functions over the course of their lives. The absence of institutional supports, such as welfare agencies, unemployment compensation, and Social Security, added to the pressures imposed on family members.

Families and individuals had to rely on kin assistance as their essential social base. Kin assistance was crucial in coping with critical life situations, such as unemployment, illness, or death, and with regular life-course transitions. The absence of dramatic transitions to adult life allowed for a more intensive interaction among different age groups within the family and the community, thus providing a greater sense of continuity and interdependence among people at various stages in the life course.

After the turn of the century, as greater differentiation in stages of life had begun to develop and as social and economic functions became more closely related to age, a greater segregation between age groups emerged, first in the middle class and later among the rest of society. This trend is closely related to the decline in instrumental relations among kin, with replacement by an individualistic and sentimental orientation toward family relations, and has led to an increasing isolation of the elderly (Hareven, 1982).

INTERDEPENDENCE AMONG KIN

Interdependence and mutual assistance involved extended kin as well. Kin served as the most essential resource for economic assistance and security and carried the major burden of welfare functions for individual family members. Contrary to prevailing myths, urbanization and industrialization did not break down traditional kinship ties and patterns of mutual assistance. Historical studies have documented the survival of viable functions of kin in the nineteenth century, especially their critical role in facilitating migration, finding jobs and housing, and assisting in critical life situations (Anderson, 1971; Hareven, 1978).

In a regime of economic insecurity, where kin assistance was the only constant source of support, family needs dictated that individual choices be subordinated to familial considerations. Individuals' sense of obligation to their kin was a manifestation of their family culture, a commitment to the survival, well-being, and self-reliance of the family, which took priority over individual needs and personal happiness. Autonomy of the family, essential for self-respect and good standing in the neighborhood and community, was one of the most deeply ingrained values (Hareven, 1982). Mutual assistance among kin, although involving extensive exchanges, was not strictly calculative. Rather, it expressed an overall principle of reciprocity over the life course and across generations. Individuals who subordinated their own careers and needs to those of the family as a collective unit, even if they were not cheerful about their sacrifice, did so out of a sense of responsibility, affection, and familial obligation, rather than with the expectation of immediate gain (Hareven, 1982).

GENERATIONAL SUPPORTS OVER THE LIFE COURSE

Close contact and mutual exchanges among parents, their adult children, and other kin persisted throughout the nineteenth century and survived in various forms in the lives of working-class and ethnic families into the twentieth century. Parents expected their grown children to support them in their old age in exchange for a variety of services they themselves had rendered their children earlier in life. Societal values rooted in their respective ethnic cultures provided an ideological reinforcement for these reciprocal relations.

Adult children's involvement with the care of their aging parents was closely related to their earlier life-course experiences, to their ethnic and cultural traditions, and to the historical context affecting their lives. Routine assistance from children to aging parents set the stage for the children's coping with subsequent crises, such as a parent's widowhood and dependence in old age. Despite a strong tradition of kin assistance among various relatives, children carried the main burden of caretaking. More distant kin provided sociability and occasional help, but the major responsibilities fell on the children, usually on one child.

The pervasive custom of the residential separation between generations in American society was modified in cases of emergency or chronic illness, handicap, or dementia among aging parents. Children, most commonly daughters, took a parent into their own household only under circumstances of extreme duress—when parents were too frail to live alone or when they needed help with their daily activities and regular care. There was no prescribed rule as to which child would become a "parent keeper." If the child was not already residing with the parent, the selection was governed by that particular child's ability and willingness to take the parent in, by the consent or support of the parent keeper's spouse, and the readiness of the parent to accept the plan. Most parent keepers evolved into that role over their life course; some were pushed into it through a sudden family crisis. Earlier life-course experience was, however, an overwhelming factor in the designation of a parent keeper. Children who had been involved in a closer day-to-day interaction with their parents during their own child-rearing years were also more likely than their siblings to take on responsibilities for caring for their parents.

Most commonly, the parent keeper was the child who continued to reside with a parent after the other siblings "bailed out." Even when both parents were alive, the common practice was to discourage the last daughter who remained at home from leaving and getting married, in order to ensure support in old age for the parents. This pattern was pervasive among various ethnic groups until World War II. Daughters remained in the parental home, postponed marriage until their middle age, or gave it up altogether. A caretaking daughter's decision to marry caused a great deal of tension. Under these circumstances, couples waited sometimes for decades until their parents died before they could marry.

Parent keepers fulfilled their responsibilities at a high price to themselves and, if they were married, to their spouses and other family members. Caretaking disrupted the daughter's work career, led to crowding in her household, often caused tension and strain in her marriage, and made her vulnerable in preparing for her own and her spouse's retirement and old age.

COHORT LOCATION IN HISTORICAL TIME

A comparison of two cohorts of adult children in an American industrial community reveals major differences in the caretaking of their aging parents. It provides a perspective on change over historical time and an understanding of the ways in which patterns of assistance of each cohort were shaped by the historical circumstances and cultural values affecting their lifetimes.[3]

The parent generation was born before 1900 and migrated to England to work in the Amoskeag Mills—the world's largest textile factory in Manchester, New Hampshire. The children, most of whom were born in the United States, consisted of two cohorts: the older children's cohort, born between 1910 and 1919, came of age during the

[3]This analysis of the cohorts in Manchester, N.H., is based on a larger project (see Hareven and Adams, 1993). The data gathering and analysis for this project were funded by the National Institute on Aging. The author gratefully acknowledges their support through the following grants: Research Career Development Grant (5 KO4 AG00026) and Research Grant (1 RO1 AG02468).

Great Depression; the younger children's cohort, born between 1920 and 1929, came of age during World War II (Hareven, 1982).

The parents viewed kin as their almost exclusive source of assistance over the life course. They expected their main supports in old age to come from their own children, rather than from institutions or agencies. Their belief in the self-sufficiency of the family led them to view public assistance as demeaning. As a French Canadian man put it: "Well, they didn't have the old folks' home those days like have today. In those days it was the kids that took care of the parents. Today, the old folks . . . they place them someplace. Get rid of them! Well, the kids want their liberty a little bit more, and they don't want to be saddled with the parents that are senile or sick or whatever."

The parents' reliance on support from kin rather than from public agencies was shaped by their ethnic backgrounds. Their involvement in mutual assistance with kin represented the continuation of an earlier practice of exchange relations, as well as an ideology that shaped their expectations from each other and from the younger generation. Their ideals of kin assistance were part of their tradition and formed a survival strategy carried over from their respective premigration cultures. They modified their ideology to fit the needs, requirements, and constraints imposed by the insecurities of the industrial environment.

Both children's cohorts shared a deep involvement with the care of aging parents, which was rooted in their earlier life-course experiences and was reinforced by their ethnic traditions and family culture. They were socialized with expectations and ideals similar to those of their parents, but were faced with the challenge of implementing them under different historical circumstances. They struggled to meet the values passed on by their parents, but new pressures, their own aspirations, and the emergence of bureaucratic agencies led them to modify these ideals. Both cohorts were ambivalent toward the obligation to be the almost exclusive caretakers of their aging parents. Beyond these dilemmas they held in common, there were significant differences between the two cohorts. The older children's cohort assigned the highest priority to recovering from the Depression and to staying afloat economically. For them, survival of the family as a collective unit remained the highest goal, rather than the pursuit of individual careers. Hence, they stretched their resources in order to keep aging parents within their homes and support them as long as possible.

The younger cohort, taking advantage of the economic recovery brought about by the war and of the career training and educational benefits that the young men had gained in the military service, tried to pull themselves out from a depressed, unemployed, working-class situation into a middle-class lifestyle (Elder and Hareven, forthcoming, 1992). Ironically, the younger children's cohort had been coached by their own parents to aspire to occupational advancement and to develop middle-class lifestyles. As they attained these goals, the children were also less available to their parents when they needed assistance in old age.

The younger children's cohort had made the transition to a more individualistic mode of thinking. They drew firmer boundaries between the nuclear family and extended kin. Their primary energies were directed toward their children and their own futures, rather than toward their parents. They viewed themselves as separate from their family of origin and upheld the privacy of their own nuclear family. This was also expressed in their preference for separate residence from the older generation. As Raymond Champagne (born 1926) put it: "I believe that marriage is something very sacred. It should be a husband-wife situation, nobody else . . . and I have listened when I was younger that families who took in the old people, I always felt that those people [taking in elderly parents] were not fully leading a married life....I just wouldn't want to be in their shoes, and I wouldn't want to put my children through it."

Members of this cohort expressed ambivalence over taking dependent elderly parents into their own homes. They helped their parents, principally by providing them with services and assistance rather than taking them in. They were more likely than the older cohort to place their physically or mentally impaired parents in nursing homes or to seek institutional help.

Neither the older nor the younger children's cohort was free, however, of the complexities involved in handling the problems of generational assistance. Both cohorts were transitional between a milieu of a deep involvement in generational assistance, reinforced by strong family and ethnic values, and the individualistic values and lifestyles that emerged in the post–World War II period. In this historical process, the older cohort's lives conformed more closely to the script of their traditional familial and ethnic cultures, while the younger cohort, as it Americanized, was being pulled in the direction of more individualistic, middle-class values.

HISTORICAL IMPLICATIONS

The difference in the experience of the two cohorts reflects major changes in attitudes toward generational assistance, kin relations, and familial values in American society. An increasing separation between the family of origin and the family of procreation over the past century, combined with a privatization of family life and especially the erosion of mutual assistance among kin, have all tended to increase insecurity and isolation as people age, especially in areas of need that are not met by public welfare programs.

While some of the intensive historical patterns of kin interaction have survived among some first-generation immigrant, black, and working-class families, there has been a gradual weakening of mutual assistance among kin over time. Gerontological studies insisting that kin assistance for older people persists in contemporary society have not documented the intensity, quality, and consistency of kin support that older people are receiving from their relatives (Sussman, 1959; Litwak, 1965; Shanas et al., 1968). Until we have more systematic evidence in this area, it would be a mistake to assume that kin are carrying or should be carrying the major responsibility for assistance to older people.

The contact that contemporary aged people have with kin, as Shanas et al. (1968) and others have found, may represent a form of behavior characteristic of certain cohorts rather than a continuing pattern (Hareven, 1978). The cohorts that are currently aged, especially the old-old, have carried over the historical attitudes and traditions of a strong reliance on kin prevalent in their youth, earlier in this century. Future cohorts, as they reach old age, might not have the same strong sense of familial interdependence, and they might not have sufficient numbers of relatives available on whom to rely. It would be a mistake, therefore, to leave kin to take care of their own at a time when the chances for people to do so effectively have considerably diminished.

Nor should the historical evidence about the continuity in kin relations be misused in support of proposals to return welfare responsibilities from the public sector to the family without basic additional supports. The historical experience reveals the high price that kin had to pay in order to assist each other without the appropriate societal supports. It thus offers a warning against romanticizing kin relations, and particularly against the attempt to transfer responsibility for the support of the elderly back to the family without adequate government assistance for caregiving relatives.

The major changes that have led to the isolation of older people in society today were rooted not so much in changes in family structure or residential arrangements, as has generally been argued, as in the transformation and redefinition of family functions. Changes in functions and values—especially the replacement of an instrumental view of the family with sentimentality and intimacy as its major cohesive forces—have led to the weakening of the role of kin assistance, in middle-class families in particular.

Over the nineteenth century, the family surrendered many of the functions previously concentrated within it to other social institutions. The retreat from public life and a growing commitment to the privacy of the modern middle-class family drew sharper boundaries between family and community and intensified the segregation of different age groups within and outside the family.

The transfer of social-welfare functions, once concentrated in the family, to institutions in the larger society resulted in further exacerbating the lack of needed assistance to older people. The family ceased to be the only available source of support for its dependent members, and the community—although it ceased to rely on the family as the major agency of welfare and social control—did not develop adequate substitute agencies for the care of elderly dependent people.

This shift of responsibility has generated considerable ambiguity, particularly in the expectations for support and assistance for aging relatives from their own kin. On the one hand, it is assumed that the welfare state has relieved children from the obligation of supporting their parents in old age; on the other hand, these public measures are not sufficient in the economic area, nor do they provide, in the other areas, the kind of supports and sociability that had been traditionally provided by the family. It is precisely this ambiguity and the failure of American society to consummate the historical process of the transfer of functions from the family to the public sector, and to strengthen the ability of the family to carry out its responsibilities, that has become one of the major sources of the problems currently confronting older people.

* * *

Tamara K. Hareven, Ph.D., is Unidel Professor of Family Studies and History, University of Delaware, Newark; adjunct professor of population sciences, Harvard University; and editor of the Journal of Family History.

REFERENCES

Anderson, M. S., 1971. *Family Structure in Nineteenth Century Lancashire*. Cambridge, England: Cambridge University Press.

Chudacoff, H. and Hareven, T. K., 1979. "From the Empty Nest to Family Dissolution." *Journal of Family History* 4(1): 69–84.

Demos, J., 1978. "Old Age in Early New England." In J. Demos and S. Boocock, eds., *Turning Points: American Journal of Sociology* 84 (Supplement).

Elder, G., 1978. "Family History and the Life Course." In T. K. Hareven, ed., *Transitions: The Family and the Life Course in Historical Perspective*. New York: Academic Press.

Elder, G. H. and Hareven, T. K., forthcoming (1992). "Rising Above Life's Disadvantages: From the Great Depression to Global War." In J. Modell, G. H. Elder, Jr. and R. Parke, eds., *Children in Time and Place*. New York: Cambridge University Press.

Glick, P. C., 1977. "Updating the Life Cycle of the Family." *Journal of Marriage and the Family* (February): 5–13.

Greven, P., 1970. *Four Generations: Population, Land and Family in Colonial Andover, Massachusetts*. Ithaca, N.Y.: Cornell University Press.

Hareven, T. K., 1976. "The Last Stage: Historical Adulthood and Old Age." *Daedalus American Civilization: New Perspectives* 105(4):13–17.

Hareven, T. K., 1978. "Historical Changes in the Life Course and the Family." In J. M. Vinger and S. J. Cutler, eds., *Major Social Issues: Multidisciplinary View*. New York: Free Press.

Hareven, T. K., 1981. "Historical Changes in the Timing of Family Transitions: Their Impact on Generational Relations." In J. G. March et al., eds., *Aging: Stability and Change in the Family*. New York: Academic Press.

Hareven, T. K., 1982. *Family Time and Industrial Time*. Cambridge, England: Cambridge University Press.

Hareven, T. K. and Adams, K., forthcoming (1993). "The Generation in the Middle: Cohort Companies in Assistance to Aging Parents in an American Community." In T. K. Hareven, ed., *Aging and Generational Relations in Historical and Comparative Perspective: Essays from the Delaware Conference*.

Kobrin, F. E., 1976. "The Fall of Household Size and the Rise of the Primary Individual." *Demography* (February):127–38.

Litwak, E., 1965. "Extended Kin Relations in an Industrial Democratic Society." In E. Shanas and G. F. Streib, eds., *Social Structure and the Family: Generational Relations*. Englewood Cliffs, N.J.: Prentice-Hall.

Modell, J. and Hareven, T. K., 1973. "Urbanization and the Malleable Household: Boarding and Lodging in American Families." *Journal of Marriage and the Family* 35:467–79.

Modell, J., Furstenberg, F. and Hershberg, T., 1976. "Social Change and Transitions to Adulthood in Historical Perspective." *Journal of Family History* 1:7–32.

Shanas, E. et al., 1968. *Old People in Three Industrial Societies*. New York: Atherton Press.

Smith, D. S., 1973. "Parental Power and Marriage Patterns: Analysis of Historical Trends in Hingham, Massachusetts." *Journal of Marriage and the Family* 35.

Smith, D. S., 1979. "Life Course, Norms, and the Family System of Older Americans in 1900." *Journal of Family History* 4:285–99.

Sussman, M. B., 1959. "The Isolated Nuclear Family: Fact or Fiction?"*Social Problems* 6:333–47.

Uhlenberg, P., 1974. "Cohort Variations in Family Life Cycle Experiences of U.S. Females." *Journal of Marriage and the Family* 34:284–92.

Uhlenberg, P., 1978. "Changing Configurations of the Life Course." In T. K. Hareven, ed., *Transitions: The Family and the Life Course in Historical Perspective*. New York: Academic Press.

Chapter 3

Social Demography of Contemporary Families and Aging

Christine L. Himes

The study of aging and older persons is inevitably tied to a study of families. Aging has an effect both on the role of families in the lives of the elderly and on the role of the elderly in the lives of their families. Families can be a source of emotional support, nursing care, financial assistance, and household assistance for their older members. Older family members may serve as a family's cultural or religious link, as providers of childcare, or as sources of emotional and financial support. Given this wide range of activities, the interest in the structure and function of families in the lives of older persons is not surprising.

Families are created by simple demographic processes—the mortality, fertility, marriage (and marital dissolution) of individuals. These processes vary over time, over age, and across ethnic groups, resulting in very different types of families. For many years the complexity of family structures was neglected in research, and the traditional definition of family—two parents living together with a child or children—was the norm. Family research often centered on the cyclical nature of family structure; individuals married, bore and raised children, and then spent some years together without children before the death of the spouse left them once again single individuals. More recently investigators have realized that neither of these models is a very accurate representation of the structure and nature of the majority of families, and greater attention is thus being paid to the diversity in families.

Most demographic research defines a family unit according to the definition used by the Census Bureau—a group of two or more persons related by birth, marriage, or adoption and residing together. Demographic information about families and living arrangements is collected by the Census Bureau through its Current Population Survey. The survey, begun in 1960, is conducted monthly and covers a representative sample of noninstitutionalized U.S. residents. In March each year respondents are asked special questions about their marital status, families, and living arrangements. The responses to these supplemental questions are summarized annually in two reports, *Household and Family Characteristics* (U.S. Bureau of the Census, 1991a) and *Marital Status and Living Arrangements* (U.S. Bureau of the Census, 1991b). The most current reports, containing data for 1990, serve as the source of the basic data on the current structure of families and the trends in family change discussed in this chapter.

If we examine related persons living together, then the majority of family units are of two basic types: either a married couple, with or without children, or a single parent and the parent's own children. In the United States there has been a decline over the past 20 years in the number of couple-headed family units. In 1970, 87 percent of family households contained married couples, 11 percent contained a single female householder, and the remaining 2 percent were headed by a single male. By 1990, only 79 percent of all family households were headed by couples, while 17 percent were headed by a single woman, and 4 percent by a single man. The decline in couple-headed families has been particularly apparent in the African American population. In 1970, 68 percent of African American families were made up of couples, with or without children, compared to 50 percent in 1990. Hispanic family households also have experienced declines in the percentage of couple-headed households, from 81 percent in 1970 to 70 percent in 1990.

Among the elderly the most common living arrangement for men is to be living with their wife—about 75 percent of men over age 65 in 1990 were living with their spouse. The living arrangements of women are slightly different. The greater chance of a woman outliving her husband means that elderly women are more likely than men to be living alone. This pattern becomes especially noticeable after age 75, when over one-half of all women are living alone. Older women in the African American and Hispanic populations are also less likely to live with a spouse as they age; however, the trend is not toward living alone but toward living with relatives—children, siblings, or other family members.

The Census definition of a family unit is useful since most statistics on families are collected for households, but it is not sufficient because many of a person's family members are not residents of the same household and many households consist of other types of relatives. The picture of the families of older persons can be broadened by looking at each of the demographic processes—mortality, fertility, and marriage—that affect family structure. An examination of the trends across time and differences across ethnic groups in these processes reveals their importance in explaining the variation in family structures.

MORTALITY

Life expectancy at birth has been increasing steadily in the United States (National Center for Health Statistics, 1992). For the white population, life expectancy at birth in 1940 was 62.1 years for males and 66.6 years for females. By 1989 (the latest year available) life expectancy had reached 72.7 years for white males and 79.2 years for white females. This increase in longevity has been more dramatic in the nonwhite population. Vital statistics data indicate that among the nonwhite population, life expectancy between 1940 and 1989 increased by nearly 16 years to 67.1 years for males and by 20 years to 75.2 years for females.

This lengthening life expectancy has resulted in two major changes in family structure and function. First, more generations are alive at any one time, increasing the vertical spread of families (Watkins, Menken and Bongaarts, 1987). Second, the longer life expectancy has resulted in a greater proportion of years of life spent with chronic health problems (Verbrugge, 1984; Crimmins, Saito and Ingegneri, 1989).

The vertical expansion of families increases the probabilities that an older person will have some family members living. For instance, models of the effects of increased longevity found that between 1800 and 1980 the length of time a child over age 15 spends with both parents still alive has tripled (Watkins, Menken and Bongaarts, 1987). In other work, Himes (1992) has found that rising life expectancy will increase the chances that an elderly man or woman will be living with a spouse and will have a surviving child.

Since increased longevity brings with it an increase in the number of years spent with disabilities, an older person will most likely receive any needed assistance at a later age and for a longer period of time. Family members, especially adult daughters, have been the traditional providers of care for impaired elderly (Stone, Cafferata and Sangl, 1987). The need to provide care for a parent for longer periods of time and at later ages will place a larger responsibility on other family members who may themselves be beginning to suffer from age-related impairments.

FERTILITY

Fertility trends over the past 40 years have been the subject of considerable attention. A rise in birthrates between 1945 and 1965 resulted in a very large group of children—the baby boom—who are now entering middle age. The very size of this group has focused attention on their needs and influenced political and economic decisions of the entire nation. In particular, there is concern in certain circles about the ability of the nation's Social Security system to meet the needs of this large group as it reaches retirement age. However, before retirement the members of the baby boom generation will experience the aging of their parents, who are just now entering the older ages. The influence of this experience may serve as a motivation for concentrated efforts to expand care for the elderly.

Understanding the pattern of past fertility is very important for determining the number of adult children of the elderly. The most important fertility change over time has been in the proportion of women who remain childless. There is a striking difference over time and between white and African American women in the proportion childless (U.S. Bureau of the Census, 1975). Among white women aged 65 to 69 in 1990, about 10 percent had not borne a child compared to 17.5 percent of African American women of the same age. The low birthrates during the 1930s result in an increase in the childless population at older ages. In the age group 85 to 89, 19.5 percent of white women and 28.1 percent of African American women were childless. In contrast, among woman who began childbearing during the 1950s, childlessness was rare; 7 percent of white women and 11 percent of African American women between the ages of 55 and 60 in 1990 were childless.

Current fertility patterns are also important to the families of the elderly through their effect on the numbers and age distributions of grandchildren. The recent increase in early childbearing creates young parents and young grandparents. These young parents, often single mothers, are frequently in need of greater assistance than parents who bear their children later (Tienda and Angel, 1982; Furstenberg, Brooks-Gunn and Morgan, 1987). These young parents often turn to their own parents as a primary resource for financial and emotional assistance and support (Eggebeen and Hogan, 1990).

However, there has also been an increase in late childbearing. In the 1980s birthrates for women over age 30 increased faster than at any other age (National Center for Health Statistics, 1991). This pattern creates older grandparents and a wider age range of grandchildren within families. Later ages of childbearing also increase the probability that an adult child of an older person will be responsible for the care of both an aging parent and a dependent child.

MARRIAGE

The third demographic process involved in the formation and structure of families is marriage and marital dissolution. Despite recent declines, marriage continues to be a nearly universal experience among Americans, and the vast majority of persons currently over age 65 have been married (U.S. Bureau of the Census 1991b). In 1990, only 4.9 percent of white women and 4.0 percent of white men over age 65 had never married. These percentages are slightly higher among the African American population, 5.3 percent of women and 5.6 of men had never married. The percentage of Hispanic elderly never married indicates a different type of marriage pattern: 5.4 percent of Hispanic women over age 65 have never married, a figure similar to that for white and African American populations, but only 2.6 percent of elderly Hispanic men have never married.

Although marriage rates are declining at younger ages, the proportion of the older population who have never been married has actually decreased over the past 20 years. This pattern represents the high rates of marriage that existed in the past. Groups of people reaching age 65 in the next 10 years, those age 55 to 64 in 1990, will have experienced even higher rates of marriage than those currently over age 65. However, this pattern apparently will reverse further in the future if the younger age groups continue their lower rates of marriage as they age.

Not all marriages endure into old age. Some may dissolve because of divorce or the death of a spouse. The divorce rate in the United States has generally declined since experiencing sharp increases in the late 1970s and early 1980s (National Center for Health Statistics, 1991). However, there has been little variation in the divorce rate for men and women over age 65. Among the elderly, divorce continues to be a relatively rare experience; approximately two out of 1,000 married men over age 65 will divorce each year and less than two out of 1,000 married women.

There has been a steady rise since the turn of the century in the proportion of marriages ending in divorce. Those who married during the Depression had higher-than-usual divorce rates. Marriages that took place following World War II, however, have had unusually low rates of divorce over the course of their married lives (Cherlin 1981). In projections of the proportion of marriages ending in divorce, Preston and McDonald (1979) find that marriages formed between 1920 and 1940 had about a 1 in 5 chance of ending in divorce.

Many divorced persons, particularly men, will remarry. As a result, few older persons are single because of divorce. Based on data in the Current Population Survey (U.S. Bureau of the Census, 1991b), just under 5 percent of white men and women over age 65 were divorced and unmarried in 1990. The chances of divorce are higher, and the chances of remarriage lower, in the African American population, and the proportions of older African Americans who are divorced reflect this difference; 8 percent of elderly African American men and 9 percent of elderly African American women are divorced and single.

The past high rates of marriage, coupled with lower rates of divorce, create a situation in which the current population over age 55 is more likely to have a spouse available in the household than will be the case in the future—offsetting some of the gains in longer life expectancy. The higher mortality of men and the tendency for women to marry men of an older age create a disparity in the presence of spouses for men and women. Elderly African American women are much more likely than any other group to be living without a spouse. Twenty-five percent of African American women over age 65 are living with a husband compared to 40 percent of white women and 40 percent of Hispanic women. A similar disparity is seen in the probability that an elderly African American man is living with his wife. Fifty-four percent of African American men live with a wife, while 76 percent of white men and 73 percent of Hispanic men are living with a wife.

The families of the elderly are affected not only by the rates of marriage and divorce they experience but also by the experience of their children. The trend toward later ages at marriage and lower proportions of young adults marrying results in an increase in the proportion of adult children between 18 and 34 who are living with their parents (U.S. Bureau of the Census 1991b). In 1990, 11.5 percent of young adults 25 to 34 years old lived with their parents, compared to 8 percent in 1970. Over one-half of young adults aged 18 to 24 were members of their parents' household in 1990. Most of these adult children had never married and were childless—97 percent of those 18 to 24 and 80 percent of those 25 to 34. However, 13 percent of the older age group living with their parents also had children living with them, creating three-generation, or more, family households.

Current and future patterns of divorce and remarriage will also be important in determining the nature of future family obligations between elderly parents and their children. The increase in single parent households with young children and the movement of adult children into parental homes increase the financial and emotional support given by elderly parents. On the other hand, the estrangement of children and parents following divorce suggests that noncustodial parents are likely to receive less support from children in their later years than custodial parents. Blended families of stepchildren are also likely to create dilemmas in the division among children of responsibilities to parents and stepparents.

FUTURE IMPLICATIONS

The important role that families play in the lives of the elderly motivates interest in understanding and describing the ways in which family structure might change over time. Trends in mortality, fertility, marriage, and divorce all influence the structure of families and, in turn, the structure of families has an impact on their function.

In the near future, elderly people will have a greater number of family members—a result of past decreases in mortality, high levels of fertility, and high levels of marriage. This network of family may be a strong source of support for older persons. However, the changing demographics of younger families is increasing the possibility that younger family members will turn to older members for support. Other factors, such as the increased participation of women in the labor force and the greater mobility of family members, are also likely to have an impact on the ability of families to interact and exchange support. Recent decreases in the rates of marriage and fertility, along with increasing rates of divorce, are creating more complicated family structures. Future elderly may have more vertical distribution in family members, that is, they may be more likely to have grandchildren and great-grandchildren, but each generation is likely to be smaller.

Understanding the demographic context in which families are rooted will become more important as family structures become more diverse. Past, current, and future trends influence the nature of family ties by affecting the number of kin, their living arrangements, and their relationships. The family situations of future elderly populations will be quite different from those today as a result of changes in the demographic processes that form families. These processes continue to operate throughout the lives of family members and continue to touch individuals through their effect on the lives of children and grandchildren.

* * *

Christine L. Himes is assistant professor, Department of Sociology, and research associate, Population Research Institute, Pennsylvania State University, University Park.

REFERENCES

Cherlin, A. J., 1981. *Marriage, Divorce, Remarriage*. Cambridge: Harvard University Press.

Crimmins, E. M., Saito, Y. and Ingegneri, D., 1989. "Changes in Life Expectancy and Disability-Free Life Expectancy in the United States." *Population and Development Review* 15(2):235–67.

Eggebeen, D. J. and Hogan, D. P., 1990. "Giving Between the Generations in American Families." *Human Nature* 1(3):211–32.

Furstenberg, F., Brooks-Gunn, J. and Morgan, S. P., 1987. *Adolescent Mothers in Later Life*. Cambridge: Cambridge University Press.

Himes, C. L., 1992. "Future Caregivers: Projected Family Structures of Older Persons." *Journal of Gerontology* 47(1):S17–26.

National Center for Health Statistics, 1991. "Advance Report of Final Divorce Statistics, 1988." *Monthly Vital Statistics Report* 39(12, Supplement).

National Center for Health Statistics, 1992. "Advance Report of Final Mortality Statistics, 1989." *Monthly Vital Statistics Report* 40(8, Supplement).

Preston, S. H. and McDonald, J., 1979. "The Incidence of Divorce within Cohorts of American Marriages Contracted Since the Civil War." *Demography* 16(1):1–25.

Stone, R., Cafferata, G. L. and Sangl, J., 1987. "Caregivers of the Frail Elderly: A National Profile." *Gerontologist* 27:616–26.

Tienda, M. and Angel, R., 1982. "Determinants of Extended Household Structure: Cultural Pattern or Economic Need?" *American Journal of Sociology* 87:1360–83.

U.S. Bureau of the Census, 1975. "Women by Number of Children Ever Born." *1970 Census of the Population, Final report PC(2)-3A*. Washington, D.C.: Government Printing Office.

U.S. Bureau of the Census, 1991a. "Household and Family Characteristics: March 1990 and 1989." *Current Population Reports, Series P-20, No. 447.* Washington, D.C.: Government Printing Office.

U.S. Bureau of the Census, 1991b. "Marital Status and Living Arrangements: March 1990." *Current Population Reports, Series P-20, No. 450.* Washington, D.C.: Government Printing Office.

Verbrugge, L., 1984. "Longer Life but Worsening Health? Trends in Health and Mortality of Middle-Aged and Older Persons." *Milbank Memorial Fund Quarterly* 62:475–519.

Watkins, S. C., Menken, J. A. and Bongaarts, J., 1987. "Demographic Foundations of Family Change." *American Sociological Review* 52(3):346–58.

Chapter 4

Divorced and Reconstituted Families: Effects on the Older Generation*

Colleen L. Johnson

Marriage, divorce, and remarriage are part of a reorganization process that entails a series of major changes in the family. The cleavages created in the nuclear family during this dynamic period have ramifications that affect the kinship system and ultimately the status of the older generation. While most research findings to date have focused on the impact these marital changes have had on parents and children, the effects on the flow of benefits between them and grandparents is beginning to attract interest among gerontologists. This chapter will (1) review what is known about how marital changes affect members of the older generation, specifically in their roles as parents and grandparents, and (2) analyze the grandparent generation during the process of kinship reorganization after the marital changes of their children.

Examples will come from my own research with northern California suburban families in which marital changes had recently occurred. In these mostly middle-class families, grandparents and their divorced children were both followed over a four-year period after divorce (Johnson, 1988a). The sample was divided by the ages of grandparents, with half under 65 years and half over that age. Also half were maternal and half were paternal grandparents. All divorcing

*The research on which this chapter is based was funded by the National Institute on Aging (R01 AG05348) and the National Institute of Mental Health (R01 MH35630).

individuals had children, and all grandparents lived in proximity to them.

RECENT TRENDS IN DIVORCE AND REMARRIAGE

Survey and census data, most of which report only on women, indicate that the divorce rate has peaked but remains at a high level of frequency. In fact, 56 percent of the early baby boomers have already divorced or are likely to do so in the future (Norton and Moorman, 1987). Divorce is generally a problem for young adults; the divorce rate declines continuously over the adult years. Consequently, by age 50, the rate is only one-quarter as large as that at age 20. In fact, 74 percent of all divorces occur before age 40, and very few, only 1.3 percent, occur after age 65. Virtually nothing is known about the adjustment of this very small minority who divorce in later life. It has been suggested that elderly women have more problems after a divorce than do younger ones (Berardo, 1982; Cooney, 1989; Hagestad and Smyer, 1982). Since divorce is so rare in old age, women with marital breakups may have few age peers of similar status with whom to share their problems. It is also likely that divorced women receive fewer supports from family and friends than do the widowed. In any case, intergenerational helping patterns are disturbed. A recently divorced grandparent is less likely than her married counterpart to be available to her children and grandchildren, some of whom are also likely to be divorced. Likewise, divorced children may be too distracted to provide supports to an elderly parent (Johnson, 1988c).

Demographers also predict that there will be a later age of marriage and increased numbers of women who will never marry; both trends, in combination with a high divorce rate, will affect the future family and the numbers of children in future generations who will be available to assist the elderly. Given the current rates of divorce, Norton and Moorman (1987) point out, there will be a marked decline in the numbers of women in old age who are married or widowed, while the numbers who are divorced will increase. Moreover, women in the future will spend more years as divorcees than they will as wives or widows.

The increased interest in the impact the divorces of children are having on older people focuses mainly on the reallocation of family resources. Divorce is a period of upheaval for individuals at any age, and it involves a process of profound and often stressful changes in families. On one hand, such changes could lead to parental distractions and declines in resources and competencies that ordinarily would have been directed toward intergenerational helping patterns. On the other hand, a divorce might bring the divorced into closer contact with parents as they turn to them for help.

GRANDPARENTING IN DIVORCED FAMILIES

Sociologically, divorce and the grandparent role converge at two ambiguous points in our social structure. On one hand, divorce and remarriage are events that are incompletely institutionalized. Their occurrence comes without clear guidelines as to how to behave or without ritual markers that indicate a socially regulated passage from one status to another (Johnson, 1988d). Likewise, our norms do not specify how grandparents should function in satisfying the basic needs of grandchildren, those needs that in normal times are delegated to the parents. Given the fact that a divorced child, particularly a daughter, is fulfilling functions formerly performed by two parents, the need for help is generally high.

On the other hand, researchers on grandparenting conclude that the role of grandparent is without clear normative guidelines on the allocation of responsibilities. The role has been described as sentimentalized and having a ritualized quality (Neugarten and Weinstein, 1964; Kahana and Kahana, 1970; Robertson, 1977). While the guidelines for grandparents are unclear and grandparents can voluntarily choose their course of action, they do so within the boundaries mediated by the parents (Bengtson and Robinson, 1985; Johnson, 1988b). In other words, grandparents are not free agents; they tend to consider their role as personally negotiated and situationally defined. Likewise, grandparents are generally at a stage in life where they welcome a decrease in family responsibilities; they can thus be ambivalent about substituting for parents in meeting the needs of grandchildren. Given these ambiguities, major dilemmas arise when their grandchildren need help. As one of my respondents commented, "If I do too much for my grandchildren, I might have to do it all. If I do too little, I might lose them."

In my study, the actions of grandparents varied according to their age and the ages of their grandchildren. Like most researchers, I found that younger grandparents provided economic help and practical assistance after a divorce more than did older grandparents. Consequently, grandparenting tends to be a middle-aged role and one that entails relationships with younger grandchildren. On the other side of the coin, the older grandparent has older grandchildren who no longer need day-to-day assistance and who may be independent of their families. Moreover, older grandparents may be experiencing the disabilities common in old age and may themselves be in need of help.

The grandparent role also varies by kinship relationship. Maternal grandparents are more actively involved than are paternal, so the mediator is a daughter who is more likely than a son to have custody of dependent children. Evidence indicates that the father's link to his child progressively weakens over the years, so he may no longer be able to provide his parents with access to his children of a divorce. Not surprisingly then, there is usually a decline in involvement of paternal grandparents with the passage of time after a divorce. In some cases, where a divorced son is unable to provide his parents access to his children, the parents may bypass him and personally establish an independent relationship with their former daughter-in-law.

PARENTS AND THEIR DIVORCED CHILDREN

In my study, parents played a significant role in easing the strains created by their son's or daughter's divorce (Johnson, 1988c). Almost two-thirds were in weekly or more-frequent contact, 89 percent were assisting with babysitting and other services, and 75 percent were providing economic assistance. Other divorced individuals went to their parents for advice and solace. In all, we estimated that 59 percent were dependent upon their parents in the sense that their lives would be negatively affected without such help.

After a divorce, the relationships between parents and their divorcing children are commonly renegotiated (Johnson, 1988c). In my study, three types of solidarities were observed to result from the reorganization process. First, increased emphasis on the solidarity of the generational bond occurred in 38 percent of the families. It entailed strengthening the blood relationship between parents, the adult child, and the grandchildren. In this case, the divorce resulted in some return to dependency upon parents and an increased flow of aid from them. Such a transition (or some would say, regression)—returning to the parents—is incongruent with our culture's most treasured norms, the norm of noninterference on the parents' part and the norm of independence on the part of the child. Where these norms are endorsed, there is a conflict between the need to depend upon a parent for some help and the desire to be independent. In the process, expectations regarding roles and relationships may be revised, and patterns of reciprocity may change.

If the parents come to the assistance of a divorcing child, the shield of privacy around the child's life is generally lowered. In the course of helping their child, parents have the opportunity to observe their child's activities and comment on her or his child-rearing practices and household management. Parents can also infer other aspects of their child's lifestyle, such as dating and sexual practices. In keeping with the norm of noninterference, however, most parents are indirect about their comments and advice to their child if they want to preserve a cordial relationship. Over time, most of the divorced children who had strengthened their generational tie had stabilized their lives. In doing so, they were eventually able to establish more independence from their parents. Over the four years, they generally drew away from their parents and reasserted the primacy of their own nuclear family.

In the second pattern of reorganization, 27 percent of the divorced children struck out alone and retained the private, bounded, but abbreviated nuclear family. After a divorce, their parents respected the privacy of the adult child's household and rarely intruded in his or her life. Consequently, the intergenerational bond was characterized by "intimacy at a distance." In these families, the parent-child relationship was likely to be distant and sometimes conflictual. Contacts were infrequent, and "we bend over backwards not to intrude in each other's lives" was the prevailing attitude. Also, this group was financially better off than the rest of the sample, so they could afford to seek help outside their family of origin. They were also likely to have more close friends in whom they confided. Not surprisingly, more individuals in this category either remarried or had a lover over the course of the study than did those who had a strong generational tie.

Third, loose-knit social networks resulting from a divorce occurred in 35 percent of the cases. With these permissive and flexible individuals, conventional family units were sometimes difficult to identify, because there was a blurring between relatives by blood, marriage, divorce, and remarriage. Relationships with relatives of divorce continued as new relationships were formed with remarriage. These patterns will be described in more detail below, but here the parent-child relationship becomes flexible and diffused. As one man commented, "My mother and I have a mellow relationship." These relationships were sustained on the basis of "liking" and personal preferences rather than norms of responsibility.

RECONSTITUTED FAMILIES

Over the years, these families experienced frequent marital changes, and during the process, the older generation commonly retained some relatives of divorce at the same time that they accumulated new in-laws with their child's remarriage. Dependent children generally are the connecting link facilitating contacts between relatives of divorce and remarriage. These relatives occupy positions along divorce and remarriage chains that are three generations deep, and new linkages, disconnections, and relinkages are continually being made.

Forty-eight percent or almost one-half of the sample of grandmothers had expanded kinship networks after a child's divorce (Johnson and Barer, 1987). The expanding networks were more common among paternal grandparents, who were far more likely than maternal grandparents to retain a relationship with their child's former spouse. The oldest generation potentially can have expanding kin networks from three sources.

1. In-law Coalitions

A grandparent's kinship system expands when relationships with their child's former in-laws are retained, and new relatives are added with their child's remarriage. In this case, members of the grandparent generation affirm the bond with their former child-in-law by emphasizing their shared biological linkage to the grandchildren. For most grandparents, it is difficult to sever a relationship with a child's former spouse: a former daughter-in-law might no longer be a son's wife, but she remains the mother of their grandchild. Thus paternal grandparents, particularly, preserve the in-law relationship in order to retain their access to grandchildren. In some cases, the mother-in-law/daughter-in-law bond becomes so close that it causes conflicts between mother and son. When a former daughter-in-law remarries, she takes their grandchildren into a new kinship unit. If grandparents recognize the shared biological linkage to the grandchildren, they strive to stay in contact with their former daughter-in-law and their grandchildren. In the course of attending birthday parties or graduations of their grandchildren, they are likely to meet the daughter-in-law's new children and stepchildren. In any case, the divorces and remarriages of children usually resulted in expanded kinship networks with the older generation as beneficiaries.

2. Divorces and Remarriages of Multiple Children

With the divorces and remarriages of several children, new subsets of in-laws accumulate. Some older people have busy lives managing a complex kinship system created by frequent marital changes of more than one child. If mothers of sons intend to stay in contact with their grandchildren, that is their only alternative. As grandparents stay involved in the life of former daughters-in-law, they remain in contact with their grandchildren. At the same time, their sons probably have remarried and acquired step and biological children. When daughters remarry, maternal grandmothers may accumulate relationships with their grandchildren's stepsiblings and the new siblings. Some grandparents include stepgrandchildren in their category of grandchildren—a practical attitude since they see them in the course of relating to their own grandchildren.

3. Two-Generation Divorce and Remarriage Chains

With widowhood or divorce, grandparents too are likely to remarry. In doing so, they potentially add another set of step and in-law relations to their networks. In these cases, the kinship network is the most expansive. One might conclude that these are divorce-prone families, many of whom have liberal and permissive values regarding family life. While in some cases considerable conflict inhibits interactions, in others cordial relations with ex-spouses and ex-in-laws are evident. During life passages such as graduations and weddings of grandchildren, these relatives meet to honor the occasion.

CONCLUSIONS

Divorce is a stressful life event for the parties involved. As this chapter attempts to demonstrate, in many cases it changes the status and roles of the older generation. In some families, there are positive outcomes. The grandparents in divorcing families intervene to assist their child and their grandchildren to the extent that some harmful effects of divorce are ameliorated, and in the process, grandparents restore more content to their roles. Mostly these grandparents are younger and healthier; they are also maternal grandparents who have easy access to their grandchildren. Since the grandparent role is mediated by the parents, it is easier to deal with their own blood relative. The situation for parents of sons is more complicated, for the person through whom they receive access to their grandchildren is a former in-law. If the divorce has been a stormy one, a son might not be able to renegotiate his parents' status and role with his children.

On the negative side, in some situations, divorce deprives grandparents of their relationship with grandchildren. Divorce may also deprive older and sicker grandparents of their child's support. If that child has been recently divorced, he or she may be too distracted to come to a parent's assistance. Given the fact also that many older people disapprove of divorce in general, its occurrence in their family is a source of conflict between generations.

An examination of remarriage and reconstituted families reveals a situation with even greater possibilities for grandparents. From the point of view of the older generation, children's remarriages enlarge their kinship network with the addition of new in-laws of remarriage and the retention of in-laws of divorce. It is here that the flexibility of our kinship system and the elasticity of its boundaries result in positive benefits to older people.

Such results may not be found in more traditional families, which have more clear-cut distinctions between relatives by blood and by marriage. However, these results are consistent with the changes in the past few decades, with their relaxation of sexual and gender constraints. In some subcultures, moreover, such flexible kinship systems are common. For instance, older African Americans benefit in regard to their social supports from just such networks in which they have freedom to mold their relationships to suit their needs (Burton and Dilworth-Anderson, 1991; Johnson and Barer, 1990). Our contemporary family and kinship system is perhaps moving in such a direction—a latent web of relationships can be activated when needed (Riley, 1983).

*　　*　　*

Colleen L. Johnson, Ph.D., is professor of medical anthropology, Medical Anthropology Program, University of California, San Francisco.

REFERENCES

Bengtson, V. And Robertson, J., eds., 1985. *Grandparenthood*. Beverly Hills, Calif.: Sage.

Berardo, D. J., 1982. "Divorce and Remarriage at Middle Age and Beyond." *The Annals of the American Academy of Political and Social Science* 464: 132–39.

Burton, L. M. and Dilworth-Anderson, P., 1991. "Intergenerational Family Roles of Aged Black Americans." *Marriage and Family Review* 16:311–22.

Cooney, T.M., 1989. "Co-Residence with Adult Children: A Comparison of Divorced and Widowed Women." *Gerontologist* 29: 779–84.

Hagestad, G. O. and Smyer, M. A., 1982. "Dissolving Long-Term Relationships: Patterns of Divorcing in Middle Age." In S. Duck, ed., *Personal Relationships*. New York: Academic Press.

Johnson, C. L., 1988a. *Ex Familia: Grandparents, Parents and Children Adjust to Divorce*. New Brunswick, N.J.: Rutgers University Press.

Johnson, C. L., 1988b. "Active and Latent Functions of Grandparenting during the Divorce Process." *Gerontologist*. 28: 185–91.

Johnson, C. L., 1988c. "Post-Divorce Reorganization of the Relationship between Divorcing Individuals and Their Parents." *Journal of Marriage and the Family* 50:221–31.

Johnson, C. L., 1988d. "Socially-Controlled Civility: Family and Kinship Relations during the Divorce Process." *American Behavioral Scientist*. 31(6): 684–701.

Johnson, C. L. and Barer B., 1987. "American Kinship Relationships with Divorce and Remarriage." *Gerontologist* 27(3): 330–35.

Johnson, C. and Barer, B., 1990. "Families and Social Networks among Older Inner-City Blacks." *Gerontologist* 30: 726–33.

Kahana, E. and Kahana, B., 1970. "Grandparenthood from the Perspective of the Developing Child." *Journal of Aging and Human Development* 2:261–68.

Neugarten, B. and Weinstein, M. S., 1964. "The Changing American Grandparent." *Journal of Marriage and the Family* 26: 199–204.

Norton, A. J. and Moorman, J. E., 1987. "Current Trends in American Marriage and Divorce." *Journal of Marriage and the Family* 49: 3–14.

Riley, M., 1983. "The Family in an Aging Society." *Journal of Family Issues* 4:439–54.

Robertson, J., 1979. "Grandparenthood:A Study of Role Conceptions." *Journal of Marriage and the Family* 39: 165–74.

Chapter 5

Dating and Courtship in the Later Years: A Neglected Topic of Research

Lori J. McElhaney

Most research on families in later life centers on increasing our understanding of the continuation and termination of long-term relationships. The body of research on widowhood is substantial, and there is a growing interest in long-term marriages that end in divorce. However, there has been a paucity of research on the development of new intimate relationships—dating, courtship, and remarriage—following widowhood or divorce in later life. Although families form and re-form across the life span, these issues are often overlooked or forgotten by researchers who study later life families.

When dating and courtship are mentioned, most people tend to think about older adolescents and young adults. This image is reflected in social science research, which typically focuses on young, never-married individuals. The dating experiences of older, previously married individuals have largely been ignored. With the growth in the older population and increases in the number of single elderly, this phenomenon may be encountered more often by professionals in the family and aging fields. The purpose of this chapter is to provide an overview of the existing research on dating and courtship in later life, concentrating on estimates of the number of older adults who are dating, social attitudes, differences between younger and older adults, the ways in which older people meet dating partners, predictors of dating, motives and functions of dating, and activities of dating.

NUMBER OF OLDER ADULTS WHO ARE DATING

There is no good estimate of the number of older adults who are dating. Although her work was not restricted only to older ages, Lopata (1979) found that only 22 percent of widows reported having close male relationships since their husbands' death. Of those, the majority (two-thirds) reported having only one close male relationship, and many married their first "boyfriends."

More recently, Bulcroft and Bulcroft (1991) examined the prevalence of dating on the basis of a subsample of previously married single adults age 55 and over from the National Survey of Families and Households. Thirty percent (93 out of 310) of the males and 6.7 percent (77 out of 1,111) of the females reported having one or more dates during the past month. Of those dating, over half the men and almost one-third of the women reported dating more than one partner in the past year. Almost one-half of both men and women identified the relationship as "steady dating."

SOCIAL ATTITUDES

An extensive assessment of social attitudes toward later life dating is not easily found. McKain (1969) states that courtship among the elderly is more influenced by outside factors than it is among younger couples. Using advice books for the elderly as an indication of changes in social attitudes, Arluke, Levin and Suchwalko (1984) report that, ironically, "although sexual activity among the elderly is being encouraged more, . . .remarriage and dating continue to be denied or discouraged for the elderly" (p. 418). Only 10 percent of these advice books published prior to 1970 approved of dating in later life. In the post-1970 advice books, the approval rate increased, but only to 24 percent. There was no difference in approval of remarriage, which stayed at 26 percent in both pre- and post-1970 books.

In a recent analysis of network television programs in which the central characters are elderly, Bell (1992) reports that despite the increase in positive images of elderly characters, "prime-time television doesn't seem to know how (or wish) to handle a continuing intimate relationship between two elderly people of the opposite sex" (p. 310).

DIFFERENCES BETWEEN YOUNGER AND OLDER ADULTS

Bernard (1956) acknowledged a difference in love between younger and older individuals. New relationships in later life can provide an opportunity to express emotions that may have been lost or suppressed during the first marriage, and love "is likely to have wider dimensions than love in youth and may perhaps be treasured even more, because the partners have experienced the deprivation of love" (p. 124).

Researchers have suggested other ways in which dating relationships are different for the two age groups. First, older daters are not experimenting with marital roles; they have most often been married before and have specific expectations for marital partners. Second, more emphasis is placed on companionship by older daters. Although less emphasis is placed on romance and sexuality, these still are a part of the dating relationship (Bulcroft and Bulcroft, 1985; Bulcroft and O'Connor, 1986; Bulcroft and Bulcroft, 1991).

Another difference is outside influences. Instead of being influenced by parents, older daters may be more influenced by the reactions of their adult children to their dating behavior (Bulcroft and Bulcroft, 1991). Sometimes the true nature of the relationship is kept hidden from children. However, Bulcroft and O'Connor (1986) suggest little influence of adult children on parent's dating but possible influence on its seriousness.

MEETING DATING AND MARRIAGE PARTNERS

Researchers have found differences between ways that widowed women meet men they merely date and ways they meet men they end up marrying. Lopata (1979) reports that, most commonly, widows meet dating partners in public places or through introductions by friends (25% each). Few dating partners knew each other in the past or through the late husband. None of the widows met dating partners through introductions by their children. This differs from the way in which new husbands were met. New husbands were more often known in the past or known through organizations and clubs (Lopata, 1979). This type of meeting of new spouses was also found by Vinick (1978) and McKain (1969).

Bulcroft and Bulcroft (1985) reported that dating partners were more often met through formal structures rather than through friends or by chance meeting. However, this seemingly contradictory finding is not surprising since the 10 adult participants in their study were identified by their membership in a singles club for older adults.

PREDICTORS OF DATING IN LATER LIFE

Activity level is important in meeting new people with whom to form intimate relationships. Older adults who are socially active have more opportunity to meet people who might be potential dating and marriage partners (Vinick, 1978).

Bulcroft and Bulcroft (1991) tested several predictors of whether or not older adults dated. For males and females combined, significant negative relationships were found for age and single family residence. Significant positive relationships were reported for comparative health, driving ability, organizational memberships, and contacts with siblings. Gender was also significant, with males more likely to date than females. The researchers did not find significant effects for marital history, contacts with children, disability level, or religious activities.

MOTIVES AND FUNCTIONS OF LATER LIFE DATING

One of the main questions asked by the researchers is why older people date. Reasons given for dating include selection of a marital partner and maintenance of social activity. In addition, for older women, dating increases prestige. Older women who date report that other women envy their dating relationship. Dating may also serve to increase self-esteem; the women feel desirable because of their ability to attract men. For men, however, dating functions as an outlet for self-disclosure (Bulcroft and Bulcroft, 1985; Bulcroft and O'Connor, 1986). For both men and women, the roles performed in dating relationships include friend, confidant, lover, and, to a lesser extent, caregiver (Bulcroft and O'Connor, 1986).

ACTIVITIES OF LATER LIFE DATING

Jacobs and Vinick (1979) report that new and developing relationships in late life tend to follow traditional gender role patterns. For example, men typically initiate and sustain the relationship. A traditional gender role pattern was also reported in a small qualitative study by Bulcroft and Bulcroft (1985).

Dating activities of widows reported in Lopata (1979) include going out to dinner, going to movies and other public places, participating in or going to sports events, and going to each other's homes. McKain (1969) describes courtship activities among retirement remarriage couples as visiting children, attending church, going to movies, attending social events, and having dinner at one partner's house. Activities reported by Bulcroft and Bulcroft (1985) included dancing, playing cards, camping and canoeing, going out or to the other's home for dinner, taking trips, and attending movies, theater, or concerts.

CONCLUSIONS

Despite the limited research on dating and courtship in later life, some implications for older adults and their families are evident. Given the imbalance in the sex ratio and the tendency for men to be involved with younger women, dating may not be a realistic option for older women. If dating is a realistic and desired activity, then staying socially active and involved in organizations increases the chance of developing new intimate relationships. The roles of other family members are not clear. Whether a person had children was not found to predict dating behavior, yet children may influence how far new relationships develop.

Given the increase in the number of single elderly people and the typical loss in social roles with aging, dating and courtship can be an important aspect of social relationships in later life. More reliable and accurate information is needed before professionals can be prepared to help families facing this issue. By ignoring the development of new intimate relationships in later life, researchers may continue to contribute to negative stereotypes of single elderly people.

*　　*　　*

Lori J. McElhaney, M.S., is a doctoral candidate in human development and family studies and a National Institute on Aging predoctoral fellow at Pennsylvania State University, University Park.

REFERENCES

Arluke, A., Levin, J. and Suchwalko, J., 1984. "Sexuality and Romance in Advice Books for the Elderly." *Gerontologist* 24(4): 415–18.

Bell, J., 1992. "In Search of a Discourse on Aging: The Elderly and Television." *Gerontologist* 32(3): 305–11.

Bernard, J., 1956. *Remarriage: A Study of Marriage.* New York: Dryden Press.

Bulcroft, K. and Bulcroft, R., 1985. "Dating and Courtship in Late Life: An Exploratory Study." In W. A. Peterson and J. Quadagno, eds., *Social Bonds in Later Life: Aging and Interdependence*. Beverly Hills, Calif: Sage.

Bulcroft, K. and O'Connor, M., 1986. "The Importance of Dating Relationships on Quality of Life for Older Persons." *Family Relations 35*: 397–401.

Bulcroft, R. and Bulcroft, K., 1991. "The Nature and Functions of Dating in Later Life." *Research on Aging 13*(2): 244–60.

Jacobs, R. H. and Vinick, B. H., 1979. *Re-engagement in Later Life: Re-employment and Remarriage*. Stamford,Conn.: Greylock.

Lopata, H. Z., 1979. *Women as Widows: Support Systems*. New York: Elsevier.

McKain, W. C., 1969. *Retirement Marriage*. Storrs, Conn.: Storrs Agricultural Experiment Station.

Vinick, B. H., 1978. "Remarriage in Old Age." *Family Coordinator 27*(4): 359–63.

Chapter 6

Elders in Southeast Asian Refugee Families

Barbara W. K. Yee

For the elderly in Southeast Asian refugee families, the experience of aging in America is very different from what they had expected for their second half of life. These elderly Southeast Asian refugees must cope with their rapidly acculturating younger family members, while having to take on different roles and expectations in a frighteningly foreign culture. The gap between the American experience of age, gender, family, and work roles and that of Southeast Asian cultures highlights just a few major differences. Life-course issues such as historical context upon migration, life stage, age at immigration, and acculturation opportunities will have a significant impact upon the adjustment and aging of these immigrants in America. Waves of Southeast Asian refugees who have come to American shores have differed dramatically, for example, in social class or urbanization, and these differences have influenced survival skills and adaptation to American life in predictable ways.

A large majority of middle-aged and elderly Southeast Asian refugees either migrated with their families or joined their relatives through the family reunification program. As a result, there are very few Southeast Asian elders in the United States who have no relatives here. Yet, the large extended family system, traditional in Vietnam, has large holes for Southeast Asian families living in America. Family reunification is the major goal for many Southeast Asian families, especially family elders.

As suggested in Gelfand and Yee (1992), the fabric of aging in America will become increasingly complex and diverse. The influences of new cultures will be woven into the American culture by immigrants. These new Americans will, over time, incorporate varying degrees of American culture within themselves and their families. The trend into the year 2000 will be increasing diversity of the aging (Gelfand and Yee, 1992) and general population (Sue, 1991). Our understanding of this diversity will enhance our ability as a society to successfully address the beautiful mosaic of elders in the future.

The purpose of this chapter is to examine the cultural transformation of the Southeast Asian refugee family as seen from the perspective of the older generation. The story is only beginning to be told. A closer examination of these rapid changes in the Southeast Asian refugee family must be made because they have major implications for elders in these families. Changes in age and gender roles and in intergenerational relationships have occurred within Southeast Asian refugee families after migration to this country. This chapter will examine the impact of these significant changes on the elder Southeast Asian refugee ("elder" as defined by this cultural group includes both middle-aged and elderly family members).

AGE ROLES

Many younger Southeast Asian refugee elders may also find that they are not considered elderly by American society. Migration to a new culture changes the timing and definitions of life stages across the life span. For instance, in the traditional Hmong culture, one can become an elder at 35 years of age when one becomes a grandparent. With grandparent status, these elder Hmong can retire and expect their children to take financial responsibility for the family. Retiring at 35 years of age is not acceptable in this country (Yee, 1989).

There is a strong influence of Confucianism in traditional Vietnamese society (Liem and Kehmeier, 1979). Confucius instituted the Cult of Ancestors, which is reflected in filial piety and respect for the family elders. Age roles within society and the family were hierarchical, with strict rules for social interaction. The child was to have total obedience to the father and to venerate him; the same was true for the relationship between a woman and her father—and later her husband—and for the student/teacher relationship. The major discrepancy for refugee families is between the traditional roles of elders in the homeland and those available to them in the United States (Weinstein-Shr and Henkin, 1991).

Weinstein-Shr and Henkin find that because the older refugees lack facility with the English language and American culture, their credibility is decreased when advising younger family members about important decisions. As younger family members take on primary roles as family mediators with American institutions—the school or legal system and social service agencies, for example—elders gradually lose some of their leadership roles in the eyes of the family and the larger American society (Yee, in press).

Weinstein-Shr and Henkin also recognize that the older refugees try to maintain their role as transmitters of traditional values and customs, but grandchildren often reject their cultural heritage in order to lessen their cognitive dissonance during acculturation to American ways. The majority of refugee families are still struggling to survive in the work and educational arenas so that they can support dependent family members. This translates into very little time left to show respect toward family elders (Detzner, in press).

Some research in other Asian-American groups, however, shows an increased interest in and appreciation of cultural roots during the adolescent and young adult period by some Asian-Americans (see review in Kitano and Daniels, 1988; Sue, D. W. and Sue, D., 1990). A so-called search for cultural roots occurs during critical periods of the life span, when people look for components of their identity. During this phase, the family elders may be called upon to help younger family members explore, discover, and appreciate their cultural heritage and family history.

Although older refugees provide childcare assistance and perform household duties for their families (Detzner, in press), they can no longer offer financial support, land, or other material goods as they would have in the homeland. The refugee process strips away the refugee elders' resources, one of the bases for high status and control of inheritance in the family. What is more important, elderly refugees can no longer provide advice and lend their wisdom: Because their counsel is derived from traditional culture and tied to the homeland, it is too foreign to American ways. Older refugees find that they are increasingly dependent upon their children and grandchildren for help rather than the reverse (see review in Yee, 1989). This role reversal between the elder and young generation has created numerous family conflicts in the Southeast Asian refugee communities (Yee, in press).

INTERGENERATIONAL ROLES

Tran (1991) found that elderly refugees who lived within the nuclear or extended family had a better sense of social adjustment than those living outside the family context. Of elderly living in a family context, those living in overcrowded conditions or in homes including children under the age of 16 experienced a poorer sense of adjustment. The relationship between overcrowding and life satisfaction holds regardless of age and across numerous groups. The relationship between living with younger children and poorer adjustment for the Southeast Asian elderly may be, as Tran speculates, a result of more economic pressures and stressors found in households with younger children. Tran's second speculation is that intergenerational conflicts among three generations living under the same roof create great stress because the younger generations are very Americanized. This acculturation gap leads to greater conflicts among the generations and depresses satisfaction with or adjustment to the refugee elders' new life because their general life satisfaction is closely tied to satisfaction with family relationships (Gelfand, 1982; Yee, in press). The age of these refugees was also inversely related to poorer adjustment. Older refugees have poorer adjustment than their younger counterparts (a finding that as been replicated in other studies) because older refugees experience more losses and fewer gains after coming to America than do their younger family members (Yee and Nguyen, 1987).

In a recent study, Rick and Forward (1992) examined the relationship between level of acculturation and perceived intergenerational differences among high school students from Hmong refugee families. These authors found that students perceived themselves to be more acculturated than their parents. Higher acculturation was associated with higher perceived intergenerational differences. Rick and Forward examined three specific acculturation items concerning the elderly: consulting the elderly on life issues, taking care of the elderly, and respecting the elderly. It appears that values concerning relationships with family elders may be the last to change, if at all, following changes in decisions about timing of marriage, having children, appropriate dress, where to live before marriage, ideal family size, or decisions on marriage.

GENDER ROLES

Refugee elders must cope with the gender role differences practiced in the homeland versus those in the United States. Even before migration, traditional gender roles were changing in Southeast Asia during the Vietnam war. Men of military age were away fighting the war, and their spouses were solely responsible for tasks normally divided along gender lines. When Vietnamese came to this country, changes in traditional gender roles sped up and became more dramatic. This was especially true for middle-aged and employed refugees. There were more employment opportunities for younger refugees and middle-aged refugee women because their employment expectations often fit with the lower status jobs that were among the few opportunities open to refugees with few English skills and little or nontransferable educational credentials. Age bias against older men and women may be operating as well, and many elders could not find gainful employment outside the home. Many middle-aged women and younger refugees of both sexes became family breadwinners. This was a radical change for the male elders, who had been the major breadwinners of the family.

The body of empirical and anecdotal work on adaptation and adjustment of refugee populations suggests that there might be a gender difference in short- versus long-term adaptation (see review in Yee, 1989). It appears that at least for short-term adaptation, which includes the period soon after migration to as long as 15 years, middle-aged and elderly refugee women adapt to life in the new country in a more positive manner than do men of the same age. Several investigators have attributed this gender difference to the continuity of female roles from the homeland to America (Yee, 1989; Detzner, in press; Barresi, 1992). Female refugee elders perform important but not necessarily honorific roles in the family such as household tasks and childcare, whereas male refugee elders, especially the old men, have less clear functional roles in the family. This latter pattern is especially evident for Cambodian men (Detzner, in press).

The ability of refugees to perform work roles outside the family also shows a gender pattern (see review in Yee, in press). There is an expansion of work roles for both young adults and young middle-aged refugee women, which is especially true for the Vietnamese group. The down side is that both groups must also take on roles and responsibilities they had not anticipated for these periods in the life cycle.

By contrast, there is a constriction of work and family roles for refugee men, especially middle-aged and elderly men. Elderly refugee men experience a significant downward mobility. Migration created the loss of high status work, family, and community roles. Many of these refugee men are not able to recover their former status because their job skills may not be transferrable to the United States or employers may be unwilling to hire an older worker. In addition, their lack of facility in English may form an insurmountable barrier to recovering their former job status by passing American credentialing tests (Yee, in press). After struggling for many years, these elderly refugees may resign by putting all their hope in the younger generation and giving the responsibility to achieve their lifelong goals to the next generation.

The pattern for long-term adaptation of refugee elders is yet to be determined empirically, but there are indications that the long-term adaptation of female refugee elders may not be so rosy. Middle-aged and elderly refugee women are integrated within the family in the short term. These elderly women provide household and childcare services in order to free younger family from these responsibilities so that they can work one or two jobs and perhaps go to school to ensure economic survival of the family. While these elderly refugee women are helping younger members of the family succeed in America, they themselves are often isolated at home and not learning new skills, English, or knowledge about American society, with which to cope with the new environment (Tran, 1988). After the family has passed through the stage of meeting basic survival needs, these elderly women may find that they are strangers in their own family and their new country. In other words, their adult children and grandchildren have acculturated to American ways in school and work settings, yet these elderly women have had few opportunities to be exposed to mainstream American culture.

SUMMARY AND CONCLUSIONS

The elders' place and role in the Southeast Asian family in the years to come are unknown, but there are several indicators that predict increasing difficulty for elderly females refugees. The impact of ethnicity and culture on aging is a dynamic process (Barresi, 1992). It is not unidirectional and unidimensional but bidirectional and multidimensional. The immigrant from another culture is touched and transformed by American culture. This transformation varies across individuals and life contexts. Something not as well recognized, but necessarily true, is that the American culture is forever changed by its association with these new Americans. Our great nation has derived its strength, creativity, and vision from our heritage of immigrants. Let us remember and appreciate this diversity. From within this diversity comes the force that will keep America at the cutting edge in a twenty-first century global society.

* * *

Barbara W. K. Yee, Ph.D., is associate professor of clinical gerontology, Graduate Studies Department, School of Allied Health Sciences, University of Texas Medical Branch, Galveston.

REFERENCES

Barresi, C. M., 1992. "The Impact of Ethnicity on Aging: A Review of Theory, Research, and Issues." Presentation at the American Society on Aging Annual Meeting, San Diego, Calif., March 15.

Detzner, D. F., in press. "Conflict in Southeast Asian Refugee Families: A Life History Approach." In J. Gilgun, K. Daly, and F. Handel, eds., *Qualitative Methods in Family Research*. Newbury Park, Calif.: Sage.

Gelfand, D. E., 1982. *Aging: The Ethnic Factor*. Boston: Little, Brown.

Gelfand, D. and Yee, B. W. K., 1992. "Trends and Forces: Influence of Immigration, Migration, and Acculturation on the Fabric of Aging in America." *Generations* 15(4):7–10.

Kitano, H. and Daniels, R., 1988. *Asian Americans*. Englewood Cliffs, N.J.: Prentice-Hall.

Liem, N. D. and Kehmeier, D. F., 1979. "The Vietnamese." In J. F. McDermott, ed., *Peoples and Cultures of Hawaii*. Honolulu: University of Hawaii Press.

Rick, K. and Forward, J., 1992. "Acculturation and Perceived Intergenerational Differences Among Hmong Youth." *Journal of Cross-Cultural Psychology* 23(1): 85–94.

Sue, S., 1991. "Ethnicity and Culture in Psychological Research and Practice." In. J. D. Goodchilds, ed., *Psychological Perspectives on Human Diversity in America*. Washington, D.C.: American Psychological Association.

Sue, D. W. and Sue, D., 1990. *Counseling the Culturally Different: Theory and Practice*, 2d ed. New York: John Wiley & Sons.

Tran, T. V., 1988. "Sex Differences in English Language Acculturation and Learning Strategies Among Vietnamese Adults Aged 40 and Over in the United States." *Sex Roles* 19: 747–58.

Tran, T. V., 1991. "Family Living Arrangement and Social Adjustment Among Three Ethnic Groups of Elderly Indochinese Refugees." *International Journal of Aging and Human Development* 32(2): 91–102.

Weinstein-Shr, G. and Henkin, N. Z., 1991. "Continuity and Change: Intergenerational Relations in Southeast Asian Refugee Families." *Marriage and Family Review* 16:351–67.

Yee, B. W. K., 1989. "Loss of One's Homeland and Culture During the Middle Years." In R. A. Kalish, ed., *Coping With the Losses of Middle Age*. Newbury Park, Calif.: Sage.

Yee, B. W. K., in press. "Markers of Successful Aging Among Vietnamese Refugee Women." *Women and Therapy* 12(2).

Yee, B. W. K. and Nguyen, D.T., 1987. "Correlates of Drug Abuse and Abuse Among Indochinese Refugees: Mental Health Implications." *Journal of Psychoactive Drugs* 19:77–83.

Chapter 7

Extended Kin Networks in Black Families

Peggye Dilworth-Anderson

The essential attributes of culture are that it is shared and that it provides a vocabulary of symbols to express meaning ascribed to various aspects of shared social life. Culture is also cognitive, precise as well as ambiguous, and it is constantly reshaped and stretched by its users (Keith, 1990). The family within the African American culture provides a template and filter for the expression of traditions, beliefs, symbols, language, ways of thinking, and rules for interacting within black cultures. It provides the foundation for understanding what it means to be black (Spencer and Adams-Markstrom, 1990). The family also provides a window into the dynamic and static aspects of the culture that are put into play within a group as it shifts and reshapes in response to the needs of its members.

This chapter discusses the cultural emergence, meaning, and future of extended kin networks in the black community. Of major concern is the support given and received by the elderly in the extended kin network. Implicit within this discussion is the assumption that African American extended families exist because of cultural, racial, historical, political, social, and economic factors (Angel and Tienda, 1982; Manson, 1989; Mutran, 1985). It is not the intent of this chapter, however, to explain how and why such factors may influence the cultural emergence, meaning, and future of the black extended family, but to discuss extended familism with a larger context in mind (Jaynes and Williams, 1989).

WHAT IS FAMILY IN THE BLACK COMMUNITY?

The traditional black communities define family relationally. Although most kin are related by blood, this is not a requisite. Family membership is not determined only by blood but also by the nature of the relationship between individuals. Fictive kin can, therefore, be as important in the black family as those related by blood. Boundaries are also permeable and flexible in black families. People can move in and out of several families and have numerous siblings or "play" siblings and parents. The family is both temporal and stable, depending on the conditions of individuals within it and the degree to which the kin network can absorb members. These traditional families foster parent-care and the absorption of dependent and needy generations (Herkovits, 1970; Gutman, 1976). This particular orientation has served the elderly blacks very well, especially in regard to creating a mutual aid system between themselves and other members of their families.

EMERGENCE OF THE MUTUAL AID SYSTEM

The mutual aid system in extended black families is rooted within a larger cultural context that evolved from the "brother" and "sister" concept in the African American community (Frazier, 1932; Franklin, 1948). This concept emerged out of the idea of survival in a hostile and oppressive society where blacks viewed themselves as "making it" only through the concerted efforts of groups of people. This way of thinking provided a belief system and a context for extended kin relations to emerge. The individual was not socialized—nor afforded the opportunity—by his underground community and the mainstream society to "make it" on his own. Historically this can be best observed in the shared planning and execution of escapes from slavery within the underground slave community (Gates, 1976). Other communal efforts, such as the sharing of resources within and across households (Escott, 1979), rearing of children (Gates, 1976; Stack, 1974), quilt making and other folk art (Vlach, 1980), were observed in the slave community, among blacks after slavery, and to some degree in contemporary black communities. History, therefore, teaches us that shared meanings and symbols of extended familism in the black community emerged, in part, in the face of slavery, oppression, and racism.

What, then, does the mutual aid system look like in contemporary black families? Does the kin network operate to nurture, protect, and maintain needy individuals within the family? Research findings show that the mutual aid system in black families today represents many traditional values in the black community. The kin network continues to absorb needy and dependent members—using few, if any, formal services to support the family. Different generations share homes with one another, particularly among low-income single mothers with young children and their grandparents. This sharing of residences was commonplace in the black community after slavery (Frazier, 1932) and during the migration to the North in the early 1930s. In both instances, economic hardships and other oppressive conditions helped shape the need for extended family relations and interactions.

Today, economic hardships have fostered a response to survival and coping in the black community that is reminiscent of social and economic conditions of the past. As a result, extended black families provide care and support to children, older people, and other needy adult members. Aged blacks and their adult children share goods and services with one another, and adult children are their parents' primary caregivers (Martin and Martin, 1978; Mutran, 1985; Taylor and Chatters, 1991).

Mutran (1985) reports that aged blacks receive as well as give support to their extended families. They give advice and economic support to their adult children more often than do whites, and assist their children by providing services to their grandchildren. In fact, current research shows that black grandparents are playing significant roles in the parenting of their grandchildren by serving as surrogate parents (or coparents) in their socialization and rearing. Many of them share homes with their grandchildren and frequently support them financially (Foster, 1983; Hogan, Hao and Parish, 1990; Wilson et al., 1990).

Apfel and Seitz (1991) identified four parenting adaptational models among early childbearing families (parental replacement, supplement, primary parent, and apprentice) that black grandmothers have used to support their grandchildren. Each model indicates a level of grandparent involvement ranging from the replacement model of taking full responsibility for their grandchildren to the apprentice model, which includes only providing limited care and support to them. Pearson et al. (1990) found that grandmothers were important parenting agents for grandchildren regardless of the family structure in which they lived. Grandmothers did vary, however, according to family structure, in the type of involvement they had with their grandchildren. For example, the presence or absence of a child's mother or father influenced the type of grandparental involvement.

However, the ability of the black extended family to continue its system of providing support to its members will be challenged by changing demographic conditions. Black families are now faced with increasing unemployment, greater numbers of single parent households, more poverty among women, and more early childbearing families. Although these changes are evident in white families, black families experience them at a higher rate (Jaynes and Williams, 1989). For example, black males are almost three times more likely to be unemployed than are whites—11 percent and 4 percent, respectively. Furthermore, 40 percent of black as compared with 25 percent of white families have no employed person in the household. Among female-headed households, the problem is even more severe. Almost 60 percent of households headed by black females, as compared to 48 percent headed by white females, have no employed person in the household. With slightly over 50 percent of black families headed by females today, the issue of poverty among families with young children, which is related to employment, is an increasing concern. Sixty-eight percent of black female heads of household with children under the age of 18 are in poverty, as compared to 48 percent of their white counterparts. These poor black women, many of whom are unskilled, with low levels of education, and with more children to take care of as compared to white females, look to their extended family for support, especially to (given the history of their roles in the family) grandparents.

THE FUTURE OF BLACK EXTENDED FAMILIES

Given the changing—and challenging—conditions in black communities, both young and old generations will continue to need one another in order to survive (Jaynes and Williams, 1989). Thus, survival and coping strategies in extended black families will need to reflect both old and new strategies that will enhance care and support among different generations. Black mothers in the work force, many of whom are single, without adequate childcare, and earning 5 percent less than their white counterparts, will continue to need whatever financial and other assistance their extended families can offer. Like those of the past, black grandparents today remain central figures in the survival process and may assume roles to protect, maintain, nurture, and serve as role models to different generations, especially young children. Of particular concern are grandfathers who can assist with grandchildren in divorced and never-married families by serving as male role models for and caretakers of their granddaughters and grandsons. Although little is written about the supportive and caregiving roles of black grandfathers, some evidence shows that they too, like grandmothers, have played important roles in supporting the extended kin system (Jackson, 1970; Johnson, 1983; Kivett, 1991; Martin and Martin, 1978). Also, given the number of black women in the labor force, many of whom are single parents, there will be a need for grandmothers, like grandfathers, to serve as role models and socializing agents to their children. Thus, social and economic conditions of black families today suggest that black grandparents will continue to serve important roles in the lives of their grandchildren but will themselves need support in caring for and supporting their grandchildren.

For instance, older grandparents (those over age 65), like the younger women in the family, have very low incomes; many who are still employed have low-wage jobs. In addition, many have health problems and live in substandard housing (Horton and Smith, 1990). Moreover, roles that were always stressful for grandparents have become increasingly so as their adult children experience increasing rates (compared to whites) of poverty and joblessness, and as teenage fertility rates and the number of single parent households rise among blacks—along with the number of multigenerational households (Farley and Allen, 1987).

Just as changing social and economic structures in the black community are influencing who will care for the children and whether they have resources to do so, the same issues are immediate for the elderly in the family. A major concern is whether the emerging black family structure headed by single females will be resilient and resourceful enough to address the needs of dependent older parents. The concern is even more serious considering the increasing life expectancy of the black elderly, especially the old-old population who are the most dependent among the elderly. Elderly blacks currently represent about 8 percent of the aged population in American society. This population is growing at a faster rate than the white elderly, especially for black females. While the total U.S. population is expected to grow only by 18 percent between 1980 and 2000, the increase of older black females is projected at 68 percent. Black females also represent the poorest among the elderly in this society—the majority are widowed and have severe health problems (Manuel, 1988). Overall, for both older black males and females, a lifelong condition of limited education and low income has put them at a disadvantage in old age. Manuel (1988, p. 47) states: "The circumstances of older blacks are not necessarily improving. The life situation of older blacks relative to older whites is not substantially different today, and in some cases is worse, than 25 years ago, before the advent of special assistance programs."

Given the changing demographic trend in the older population and in the status of black families, it is suggested here that family caregivers of aged blacks will not be able to maintain their traditional system of mutual aid and support. Competing demands of different dependent generations in the family will greatly challenge black women's ability to care for their children and older parents. Again, young single mothers who will have a history of poverty will be the expected caregivers of the growing older population in the black community—and these single mothers will themselves need as much or more support as the aged for whom they will be expected to care. It is feasible to surmise, then, that as the structure and composition of the black family changes, the quality of life for the elderly will be challenged, thus requiring a higher level of flexibility and resiliency of individuals in the extended kin network to care for and support them. The concern, however, for black families is whether the extended kin network, given its myriad problems, can absorb the needs of older members.

SUMMARY AND DISCUSSION

One would assume that the cultural expectation in most black families is that the kin network will continue providing care and support to dependent members. However, the ability to maintain this traditional way of responding will be challenged by the status, situation, and condition of those who serve in the caregiving and supportive roles (Barresi and Menon, 1990). Changing sociodemographic characteristics of black families indicate that a large proportion of the pool of kin-keepers and caregivers will be poor and needy.

Although only limited information is available that discusses the range of responses black extended families use to address the needs of their members, inferences can be drawn from what is known. Three major inferences are noted here: (1) Cultural ways of believing and behaving will encourage the kin network to absorb its needy members.

(2) The kin system will probably become increasingly vulnerable in light of the few resources available to it to meet the multiple demands and needs of different generations. (3) Black families will attempt to reshape and redefine themselves to meet the needs of the kin network.

These observations should not invalidate the perception that black extended kin networks and systems are working for black families, especially the elderly. Instead, they point to challenges and problems black families face. It is hoped that black families in the future will become more resilient and flexible in attempting to find ways to address the social and economic conditions that threaten the existence of the extended kin network. They will probably develop diverse ways of surviving and coping. Researchers studying and practitioners working with black families need to be sensitive to the diverse ways in which black families will try to address the challenges they face. This diversity in black families may require researchers and practitioners to broaden their criteria for what constitutes the extended kin system as well as what constitutes survival and coping among kin networks. Such understanding would consider the multiplicity of demands and stressors facing black families today in attempting to support and care for the old and other needy generations within the extended kin network.

*　　*　　*

Peggye Dilworth-Anderson, Ph.D., is professor, Department of Human Development and Family Studies, University of North Carolina, Greensboro.

REFERENCES

Angel, R. J. and Tienda, M., 1982. "Determinants of Extended Household Structure: Cultural Pattern or Economic Need?" *American Journal of Sociology* 887: 1360–83.

Apfel, N. H. and Seitz, V., 1991. "Four Models of Adolescent Mother-Grandmother Relationships in Black Inner City Families." *Family Relations* 40:421–29.

Barresi, C. M. and Menon, G., 1990. "Diversity in Black Family Caregiving." In Z. Harel, ed., *Black Aged*. Newbury Park, Calif.: Sage.

Escott, P. D., 1979. *Slavery Remembered: A Record of Twentieth-Century Slave Narratives*. Chapel Hill: University of North Carolina Press.

Farley, R. and Allen, W. R., 1987. *The Color Line and the Quality of Life in America*. New York: Oxford University Press.

Foster, H. J., 1983. "African Patterns in the Afro-American Family." *Journal of Black Studies* 14:201–32.

Franklin, J. H., 1948. *From Slavery to Freedom: A History of American Negroes*. New York: Alfred A. Knopf.

Frazier, E. F., 1932. *The Negro Family*. Chicago: University of Chicago Press.

Gates, H. L., 1976. *The Classic Slave Narratives*. New York: Random House.

Gutman, H., 1976. *The Black Family in Slavery and Freedom, 1750–1925*. New York: Pantheon Books.

Herkovits, M., 1970. *The Myth of the Negro Past*. Boston: Beacon Press.

Hogan, D., Hao, L-X and Parish, W., 1990. "Race, Kin Networks, and Assistance to Mother-Headed Families." *Social Forces* 68:797–812.

Horton, C. P. and Smith, J. C., 1990. *Statistical Records of Black America*. Detroit, Mich.: Gale Research, Inc.

Jackson, J. J., 1970. "Kinship Relations Among Urban Blacks." *Journal of Social and Behavioral Sciences*. 16:1–13.

Jaynes, D. J. and Williams, R. M., 1989. *A Common Destiny: Blacks in American Society*. Washington, D.C.: National Academy Press.

Johnson, C., 1983. "A Cultural Analysis of Grandmother." *Research on Aging* 5:547–68.

Keith, J., 1990. "Aging in Social and Cultural Context: Anthropological Perspectives." In R. Binstock and L. George, eds., *Handbook of Aging and the Social Sciences*. New York: Academic Press.

Kivett, V., 1991. "Centrality of the Grandfather Role Among Rural Older Black and White Men." *Journal of Gerontology* 46:S250–58.

Manson, S. M., 1989. " Long-Term Care in American Indian Communities: Issues for Planning and Research." *Gerontologist* 29:38–44.

Manuel, R. C., 1988. "The Demography and Epidemiology of Elder Black Adults." In J. J. Jackson, ed., *The Black American Elderly: Research on Physical and Psychosocial Health*. New York: Springer.

Martin, E. P., and Martin, J. M., 1978. *The Black Extended Family*. Chicago: University of Chicago Press.

Mutran, E., 1985. "Intergenerational Family Support Among Blacks and Whites: Response to Culture or to Socio-Economic Differences." *Journal of Gerontology* 40:382–89.

Pearson, J. L. et al., 1990. "Black Grandmothers in Multigenerational Households: Diversity in Family Structure and Parenting Involvement in the Woodlawn Community." *Child Development* 61:434–42.

Spencer. M. B. and Adams-Markstrom, C., 1990. "Identity Processes Among Racial and Ethnic Minority Children in America." *Child Development* 61: 290–310.

Stack, C. B., 1974. *All Our Kin: Strategies for Survival in a Black Community*. New York: Harper & Row.

Taylor, R. and Chatters, L., 1991. Extended Family Networks of Older Black Adults. *Journal of Gerontology*, 46: S210–17.

Vlach, J. M., 1980. "Arrival and Survival: The Maintenance of an Afro-American Tradition in Folk Art and Craft." In I. Quimby and S. Swank, eds., *Perspectives on American Folk Art*. New York: W. W. Norton.

Wilson, M. N. et al., 1990. "Flexibilty and Sharing of Childcare Duties in Black Families." *Sex Roles* 22:409–25.

Chapter 8

The Role of Church and
Family Support in the Lives
of Older African Americans *

Carla T. Walls

Historically, black churches have been seen as a viable source of support for providing informal services to African Americans, because of the advocacy and extended kin roles that they have played in African American communities (Poole, 1990; Taylor, Thornton and Chatters, 1987). Recent literature suggests that the informal support offered by black churches plays a particularly important role in the lives of older African Americans. The purpose of this chapter is to examine that role, specifically, the relationship between church support, religious involvement, and psychological well-being among elderly African Americans.

First, a brief discussion of the role that black churches have played in the lives of older African Americans is presented. Second, a description is provided of a study that examines how social support in churches complements and interacts with family support. Third, the major findings are summarized. Finally, the implication of these findings for future research and service delivery are highlighted.

*This research was supported by the National Institute of Mental Health Grant No. T32 MH 18904 to Pennsylvania State University. An earlier version of this chaper was presented at the 42nd Annual Scientific Meeting of the Gerontological Society of America, Minneapolis, Minn., November 1989.

BLACK CHURCHES AS SUPPORT SYSTEMS

As in most racial minority groups, the primary source of social support for older African Americans is the family (Dressler, 1985; Chatters, Taylor and Jackson, 1986; Langston, 1980). Current research, however, suggests that older African Americans have support networks beyond their family (Cantor, 1979; Langston, 1983). This research suggests that in addition to the family, older African Americans rely on friends, neighbors, and their churches for supplemental support (Langston, 1983; Taylor and Chatters, 1986b).

Consistent with Cantor's (1979) hierarchical-compensatory model, which suggests that an ordered preference exists for those selected to provide care, older African Americans seek assistance from family members first before accepting help from others (see also Chatters, Taylor and Jackson, 1986). As a second option, older blacks turn to their churches for assistance before utilizing services from some formal agencies (Ambrose, 1977; Langston, 1983). Research indicates that African American elders rely on their church for assistance more often than do elderly whites, especially when community-based services are not available (Haber, 1984; Hirsch, Kent and Silverman, 1972). The involvement of African American elders in the church supports Antonucci and Akiyama's (1987) concept of a "convoy" of social support, since these individuals' lifetime connection to the church generates a support network that provides help when needed.

The structure and function of churches, particularly black churches, contribute to their ability to provide religious activities and a range of informal services that respond to the survival and social needs of their congregation (Taylor and Chatters, 1986a; Wilson and Netting, 1988). For example, given the structure and function of black churches, social gerontologists are beginning to explore the feasibility of churches providing health and wellness programs (Netting, Thibault and Ellor, 1988). In a three-phase community advocacy study, Tobin, Ellor and Anderson-Ray (1986) demonstrated the potential of churches to connect with the formal service delivery system. They assessed the role of churches as social service providers to the elderly in three communities—blue collar, white collar, and deteriorating inner-city neighborhoods. They found that service programs supported by groups of churches and programs sponsored jointly by churches and social service agencies did exist. They concluded that the potential for expansion of service in these areas is great.

It is important to note, however, that a study of churches as support networks or service providers must take into account that the primary emphasis of churches is religious activities. The 1988 study of Sheehan, Wilson and Marella suggests that the perceived role of the church is important in the development of church-based programs. They surveyed 212 churches and synagogues to assess factors related to program development and linkages between churches and community agencies. Churches and synagogues that perceived their role as addressing the social as well as the spiritual needs of their aging members provided more church- or synagogue-based programs. This research underscores the importance of assessing how social support in churches complements and interacts with support provided by families. The following sections of this chapter examine older African Americans' perceptions of support from their family and church as such perceptions relate to psychological well-being.

DESCRIPTION OF THE RESEARCH

The research presented here was an exploratory study involving 98 African Americans, ranging in age from 65 to 104 (mean=76 years), recruited through local black churches in an urban area of Pennsylvania. Since the churches were used as sites to gain access to the aged African Americans, descriptive information about the churches was obtained from the ministers to better understand the structure and function of the churches. Interviews were conducted with older African Americans whose ministers agreed to participate in the study.

This sample of aged African Americans was relatively healthy. Sixty percent indicated that their health was good, and 80 percent had no trouble performing instrumental activities of daily living. They had an average of 10 years of education. Fourteen percent had income that was less than $5,000 per year, 44 percent had income between $5,000 and $10,000, 25 percent had income between $10,000 and $15,000, 8 percent had income between $15,000 and $20,000, and 9 percent had income greater than $20,000 per year. Forty percent of the sample were married, 53 percent widowed, and the remaining 7 percent were either divorced or never married. Seventy-five percent were females, and 25 percent were males.

Social support, religiosity, well-being, health status, and functional health status of the respondents were measured. The Social Provision of Support scale (SPS) (Russell and Cutrona, 1984)—a 24-item instrument that measures six types of support: attachment, social integration, reassurance of worth, reliable alliance, guidance, and opportunity for nurturance—was used to measure perceived support from family and church members. Eight additional items, which measured financial and practical assistance, were taken from the Social Support Resource (SS-R) scale (Vaux and Harrison, 1985). They were combined with the guidance items of the SPS scale to form a single scale of instrumental support. The SS-R was also used to describe the social networks of the older African Americans (Vaux and Harrison, 1985). The individuals named as important or close to them were used to obtain a total network score.

Since the spiritual aspects of religion (i.e., religiosity) constitute a multidimensional variable, they were measured separately from involvement in organized church activities. The Dimension of Religion scale (King and Hunt, 1972) measured spiritual beliefs and nonorganizational religious behavior (beliefs, prayer, bible reading), and the Social Integration of the Aged in the Church scale (Moberg, 1965) measured the degree of involvement in organized religious activities.

The 17-item Philadelphia Geriatric Center Morale scale was used to measure subjective well-being (Lawton, 1975). This scale measures the components of agitation, loneliness and dissatisfaction, and attitudes toward one's own aging.

The Physical Health subscale was used to measure the health status of these African American elders (OARS, 1978). This scale measures subjective health, the presence of an illness, and the degree to which the illness is disabling. Additionally, the OARS (1978) Activities of Daily Living subscale was used to measure the individuals' capacity to care for themselves on a daily basis.

RESULTS OF THE STUDY

Most studies that examine the role of black churches as supportive networks have not considered or described how that role relates to family support and psychological well-being. In theory, when one talks about the family and the church network, the inclination is to think of them as two distinct institutions. However, these networks are not mutually exclusive. Most of the people in the networks of these African American elders were immediate family members and friends who attended their church. This finding suggests that it is important to consider the church network in relation to the family when the support networks of African American elders are studied.

One of the striking findings of this research is that family members were perceived as providing more emotional than instrumental support, compared to the perception of more instrumental than emotional support provided by church members. As expected, African American elders in this study perceived that more support overall was provided by the family than by church members; nevertheless, church support contributed to feelings of well-being.

The church and family networks were both important predictors of well-being. African American elders who received high support from either the family or the church network experienced more feelings of well-being than those who received moderate support from both networks. Additionally, older African Americans who received high levels of support from both networks scored best on well-being. Finally, the results showed that it was the perceptions the African American elders had of the church, and not the ideology (spiritual aspects) or involvement in the organizational aspects of the church, that generated feelings of well-being.

There are two possible ways to interpret these findings. One view is that in current times, black families tend to provide more emotional support, because they do not have adequate resources to provide instrumental support. In light of the fact that black churches may have more resources in comparison to what some African American families have, the churches are able to provide some instrumental support, even though it is sporadic. These findings show that older African Americans normally attend the same church as other family members, a circumstance that heightens the expectation for assistance and reciprocity, since the religious community thus becomes an extended family network (see Antonucci and Akiyama, 1987). This synthesis is beneficial for the development of supportive exchanges .

An alternative interpretation is connected to the fact that this was a sample of African American elders who were doing well physically and economically. Financial and practical assistance from the family was therefore not a necessity. Additionally, these data are dealing with people's *perceptions* of support—not actual supportive exchanges. This group of African American elders came from an era in which it was believed the church would provide help if needed. The perceptions of this cohort, then, may be different from the reality of what black churches actually provide. More research is needed to better understand the connection between perceptions and actual support from the church and how this differs across generations.

IMPLICATIONS FOR FUTURE RESEARCH

This chapter has identified the structure of support that comes from black churches. It also highlights the power that perceptions of black churches have for generating feelings of well-being. One of the clearest things this research shows is that elders' perceptions of black churches are strong, which may contribute to the ability of the churches to serve as an important resource in enhancing minority elderly's use of formal services or their ability to cope with life changes. A considerable amount of research has focused on the historical role of the black church as a buffer to psychosocial stressors (Poole, 1990; Taylor, Thornton and Chatters, 1987). Since our study comprises a relatively healthy sample of aged blacks, it does not demonstrate the buffering effects of support from church members.

Our study does, nevertheless, highlight the potential of black churches to play a more active role in the development and implementation of various health and wellness programs. Our findings are consistent with those of Sheehan and associates (1988) illustrating the powerful effect that the church's role as perceived by ministers or elderly members has on the development of church-based programs. The work suggests that the informal social components of the church may be a critical mechanism in providing support to aged blacks, supplementing the support available from the family. More research is needed, however, especially intervention research that substantiates the black church's potential to augment formal support networks and to identify factors that inhibit the formal delivery of services.

ACKNOWLEDGMENTS

The author wishes to thank Linda M. Burton for reading earlier drafts of this chapter and Michael Rovine and Pam Lautsch-Bowman for their assistance with data analysis.

*   *   *

Carla T. Walls, Ph.D., was holder of a postdoctoral fellowship, funded by the National Institute of Mental Health, in the Department of Human Development and Family Studies at Pennsylvania State University, University Park. She is currently senior research associate at Philadelphia Health Management Corporation.

REFERENCES

Ambrose, J. J., 1977. "The Black Church as a Mental Health Resource." In D. Jones and W. Matthews, eds., *The Black Church: A Community Resource.* Washington, D.C.: Institute for Urban Affairs and Research, Howard University, pp. 105–13.

Antonucci, T. C. and Akiyama, H., 1987. "Social Support Networks in Adult Life and a Preliminary Examination of the Convoy Model." *Journal of Gerontology* 42(5):519–27.

Cantor, M. H., 1979. "Neighbors and Friends: An Overlooked Resource in the Informal Support System." *Research on Aging* 1:434–63.

Chatters, L. M., Taylor, R. J. and Jackson, J. S., 1986. "Aged Blacks' Choices for an Informal Helpers Network." *Journal of Gerontology* 41(1):94–100.

Dressler, W. W., 1985. "Extended Family Relationships, Social Support and Mental Health in a Southern Black Community." *Journal of Health and Social Behavior* 26:39–48.

Haber, D., 1984. "Church-based Programs for Black Caregivers of Noninstitutionalized Elders." *Journal of Gerontological Social Work* 7:43–49.

Hirsch, B., Kent, D. P. and Silverman, S., 1972. "Homogeneity and Heterogeneity Among Low-Income Negro and White Aged." In D. P. Kent, R. Kastenbaum and S. Sherwood, eds., *Research Planning and Action for the Elderly: The Power and Potential of Social Science.* New York: Behavioral Publishers, pp. 400–500.

King, M. B. and Hunt, R. A., 1972. "Measuring Religious Dimensions: Studies of Congregational Involvement." *Studies of Social Science*, vol. 1. Dallas, Tex.: Southern Methodist University.

Langston, E. J., 1980. "Kith and Kin, Natural Support Systems: Their Implications." In E. P. Stanford, ed., *Minority Aging: Policy Issues for the 80s.* San Diego, Calif.: Campanile Press, pp. 124–44.

Langston, E. J., 1983. "The Family and Other Informal Supports." In E. P. Stanford and S. A. Lockery, eds., *Minority Aging and Long-Term Care.* San Diego, Calif.: Campanile Press, pp. 35–37.

Lawton, M. P., 1975. "The Philadelphia Geriatric Center Morale Scale: A Revision." *Journal of Gerontology* 30:77–84.

Moberg, D. O., 1965. "Religiosity in Old Age." *Gerontologist* 5(2):78–87.

Netting, F. E., Thibault, J. M. and Ellor, J. D., 1988. "Spiritual Integration: Gerontological Interface Between the Religious and Social Service Communities." *Journal of Religion and Aging* 5(1/2): 61–75.

OARS, 1978. *Multidimensional Functional Assessment: The OARS Methodology, A Manual,* 2d ed. Durham, N.C.: Duke University Center for the Study of Aging and Human Development.

Poole, T., 1990. "Black Families and the Black Church: A Sociohistorical Perspective." In H. E. Cheatham and J. B. Stewart, eds., *Black Families: Interdisciplinary Perspectives.* London: Transaction Publishers, pp. 33–48.

Russell, D. and Cutrona, C., 1984. "The Provisions of Social Relationships and Adaptation to Stress." Paper presented at the American Psychological Association convention in Toronto, Canada.

Sheehan, N. W., Wilson, R. and Marella, L. M., 1988. "The Role of the Church in Providing Services for the Aging." *Journal of Applied Gerontology* 7(2):231–41.

Taylor, R. J. and Chatters, L. M., 1986a. "Church-based Informal Support Among Aged Blacks." *Gerontologist* 26: 637–42.

Taylor, R. J. and Chatters, L. M., 1986b. "Patterns of Informal Support to Elderly Black Adults: Family, Friends, and Church Members." *Social Work* 31: 432–38.

Taylor, R. J., Thornton, M. C. and Chatters, L. M., 1987. "Black America's Perceptions of the Sociohistorical Role of the Church." *Journal of Black Studies* 18(2):123–38.

Tobin, S., Ellor, J. W. and Anderson-Ray, S. M., 1986. *Enabling the Elderly: Religious Institutions within the Community Service System*. Albany: State University of New York Press.

Vaux, A. and Harrison, D., 1985. "Support Network Characteristics Associated with Support Satisfaction and Perceived Support." *American Journal of Community Psychology* 13:245–68.

Wilson, V. and Netting, F. E., 1988. "Exploring the Interface of Local Churches with the Aging Network: A Comparison of Anglo and Black Congregations." *Journal of Religion and Aging* 5(1/2): 5–16.

Chapter 9

The Families of Older Gay Men and Lesbians

Douglas C. Kimmel

Lesbians and gay men grow older in several different types of families, which may include their family of origin, their family of spouse and children, and their family of friends and lovers.

Within these families, gay men and lesbians play important roles in the rearing and nurturing of children. Similarly, the care of elder parents in some families today is provided by lesbian or gay offspring.

Although some older gay men and lesbians have little contact with their biological families, we can describe briefly the three most typical roles of lesbians and gay men in families of one kind or another.

First, long-term relationships are much more frequent among gay men and lesbians than is commonly assumed (Peplau, 1991). The recent epidemic of aids has made this fact widely known for gay men, as the word "companion" is now published in obituaries in even such traditional newspapers as the *New York Times*. While it is currently not legal for same-gender couples to marry, many couples have some public or private ceremony, including religious celebrations. Recently, several municipalities have recognized same-gender partnerships and now provide for employees who are part of such couples some of the same benefits given to those employees who are married, including bereavement leave, health insurance, and childcare or pregnancy leave. Some major private employers also are now providing spousal health insurance and other benefits to the unmarried partners of heterosexual, bisexual, lesbian, and gay employees. (In one case, however, the company did not extend the spousal benefits to nonmarried employees with a heterosexual partner because, it was argued, those persons could marry, whereas lesbians and gays cannot.)

There are no good data on the number or proportion of older gay men and lesbians who are living in long-term partnerships, of course. Often it is assumed that lesbians are more likely to be doing so than are gay men, but there is no evidence that this is so. In one representative national sample, 60 percent of gay and bisexual men and 64 percent of lesbian and bisexual women said they were in a relationship (Hatfield, 1989). Based on my research and study of others' research on lesbian and gay aging, I would caution against any simple generalization based on gender. Race, culture, age, and individual circumstance are very influential. For example, it is easy to find white gay men who have lived together openly as a couple for over 40 years—and not just in urban areas—and there are similar lesbian couples, to be sure. In general, when matched on age and background, lesbian, gay, and heterosexual couples do not differ on standard measures of relationship quality or satisfaction (Kurdek and Schmitt, 1986; Peplau, Padesky and Hamilton, 1982). In her recent review, Peplau (1991) noted the following:

> Research has shown that most lesbians and gay men want intimate relationships and are successful in creating them. Homosexual partnerships appear no more vulnerable to problems and dissatisfactions than their heterosexual counterparts, although the specific problems encountered may differ for same-sex and cross-sex couples (p. 195).

Second, older lesbians and gay men typically live within a self-created network of friends, significant others, and selected biological family members that provides mutual support of various kinds, as a family system might do. Lipman (1986) noted previously that older lesbians and gay men tend to have more friends than do heterosexuals of similar age, and that most of those friends are of the same gender and also are lesbians or gay men. In addition, often there are younger persons who look to the older gay person as a role model and mentor. If the younger person is gay, the older person may serve as a kind of parent or grandparent figure, which is important since families of origin usually do not have such gay role models for young people; even if the younger person is not gay, the older gay or lesbian may be a role model professionally, personally, and politically (e.g., as a feminist, activist, or an example of a creative nonconformist).

Several aspects of this self-defined family network were described by respondents in my study of older gay white men (Kimmel, 1977, 1978). For example, since one cannot rely on family members for care, one must plan for aging by creating a support system. However, there is a danger of withdrawing into a self-contained world of one's peers; and unlike in a traditional family, there is a risk of not having contact with other generations, including children. Dunker (1987) made a similar observation: "It's imperative that older lesbians find younger friends. [Younger people] need us, too. The old crone, the wise woman, the witch have always been valued in many cultures. We can ensure that they are valued here, too" (p. 81).

Third, some gay men and lesbians have special roles in their family of origin that reflect their unique social position, which may take many forms. One might be the caretaker of an aging relative, selected for the job, as it were, because of being unmarried, or geographically mobile, or willing to live with an aged parent and provide care when necessary. Likewise, one might have greater access to educational opportunities or more disposable income because of not having childcare expenses. Thus, the family of origin may look to lesbian and gay members for vocational, educational, financial, or counseling support. From time to time, nephews, nieces, and other relatives may turn to the older gay or lesbian relative for help or shelter. Also, in times of crisis, the family may turn to the lesbian or gay member for emergency aid, counsel, or moral support.

CONCLUSION

Gay men and lesbians are members of families. They do grow old. And they create a variety of families as they age. They represent an important facet of the social ecology of aging, and they call attention to the significance of group differences in aging. Moreover, an understanding of cohort and generational differences between age groups sheds light on the recent dramatic changes in the lives of lesbians and gay men and in the broader society of families—of which the gay and lesbian community is an integral part.

*   *   *

Douglas C. Kimmel, Ph.D., is a professor in the Department of Psychology, City College, City University of New York.

REFERENCES

Dunker, B., 1987. "Aging Lesbians: Observations and Speculations." In Boston Lesbian Psychologies Collective, ed., *Lesbian Psychologies*. Urbana:University of Illinois Press, pp.72–82.

Hatfield, L., 1989. "Gays Say Life Getting Better." *San Francisco Examiner*, 30 June, p. A15.

Kimmel, D. C., 1977. "Psychotherapy and the Older Gay Man." *Psychotherapy: Theory, Research and Practice* 14:386–93.

Kimmel, D.C., 1978. "Adult Development and Aging: A Gay Perspective." *Journal of Social Issues* 34(3):113–30.

Kurdek, L.A. and Schmitt, J.P., 1986. "Relationship Quality of Partners in Heterosexual Married, Heterosexual Cohabiting, and Gay and Lesbian Relationships." *Journal of Personality and Social Psychology* 51:711–20.

Lipman, A., 1986. "Homosexual Relationships." *Generations* 10(4): 51–54.

Peplau, L.A., 1991. "Lesbian and Gay Relationships." In J. C. Gonsiorek and J.D. Weinrich, eds., *Homosexuality: Research Implications for Public Policy*. Newbury Park, Calif.: Sage.

Peplau, L. A., Padesky, C. and Hamilton, M., 1982. "Satisfaction in Lesbian Relationships." *Journal of Homosexuality* 8:23– 35.

Chapter 10

The Oldest-Old in Families:
An Intergenerational Perspective

Lillian E. Troll and Vern L. Bengtson

In light of current research in gerontology and family relationships, two general questions can be asked about family relationships of the oldest-old: What do families contribute to the adaptation of individuals in late-late life? What do the oldest generations contribute to their families?

One thing to remember about family relationships of the very old in contemporary American society is that they are primarily cross-generational, not same-generational. A second point is that these are intergenerational relations primarily among people who do *not* live in the same household—in contrast to the oldest-old in other societies today, especially in Asia, where intergenerational living in late adulthood is still the norm. With the exception of those few very much older Americans—mostly men—who still have living marital partners, the family relationships of those over the age of 85 involve what Litwak (1960) has called the modified-extended kind of kinship relations. Even though few of these elderly live with kin, connections to other relatives are through their children (Johnson and Troll, 1992) and grandchildren (Bengtson, Rosenthal and Burton, 1990; Troll, 1991). Thus many of those who do not have living children end up isolated.

We can address answers to the two questions above from two ongoing longitudinal studies that include the oldest-old in a family context:

(1) Colleen Johnson's University of California at San Francisco study of three waves of interviews with 150 Bay Area residents over the age of 85 (Johnson and Troll, 1992), and (2) the 20-year survey and interview study with three—and now four—generations of aging family members at the University of Southern California (Bengtson and Roberts, 1991). The San Francisco data are most relevant to the first question, and the Los Angeles data to the second.

WHAT DO FAMILIES CONTRIBUTE
TO THE ADAPTATION OF THE OLDEST-OLD?

Half the 39 men over 85 who were interviewed by Colleen Johnson and her staff at USCF were still married at the time of their first interview in 1988, but only 10 percent of the 111 women were. While half the men were still living with a wife, only one-fourth of the women lived with any family member. The other half of the men and almost two-thirds of the women lived alone. (The sample, largely selected through voting records, consisted of noninstitutionalized people.) In terms of the demography of their intergenerational relationships — what Bengtson, Rosenthal and Burton (1990) term the "opportunity structure" for possible cross-generational assistance, affection, and association—about 70 percent of both men and women had at least one living child, and 40 percent at least one sibling. When it comes to the relative significance of children and siblings at this time of life, however, the children are clearly more salient. Two-thirds of the USCF respondents saw a child at least weekly, but less than 10 percent reported seeing a sibling that often. Even if their siblings were still living, few were nearby, and many of these had as many difficulties with mobility as did the respondents.

Much gerontological family literature has focused upon the "caregiving" relationship in which children supply the needs of their aging parents and provide services like shopping, housecleaning, and even personal care (Troll, 1986). Many of the USCF respondents indicated they did not need this kind of help, at least at the beginning of the study. Nevertheless, 60 percent of the women did report receiving some instrumental support from their children. Only 30 percent of the men reported this—a spouse would be first in line to provide assistance, of course, and more of the men had a wife than did women a husband to provide such support (Gatz, Bengtson and Blum, 1990; Johnson and Troll, 1992). In this sample, 47 percent of the women's children and 11 percent of the men's could actually be called caregivers at Time-1.

Other studies have suggested that as parents get progressively more feeble, their children are more likely to provide nursing kinds of services or arrange changes in housing and monitor well-being in these new places (Archbold, 1982; Troll, 1986). However, the second round of interviewing in the USCF study did not show this kind of change. Those children who had been involved in the care of parents at Time-1 continued to be involved at Time-2; however, those who had not previously been involved did not increase their care, even though there was a steady decline in the health and independence of the respondents over time.

Since the San Francisco sample was chosen originally to include only noninstitutionalized people, few of them needed much instrumental help, at least at the time of the first interview. But what loomed large in the interview responses was the amount of "expressive support" their children gave them. Eighty percent of the women and 74 percent of the men mentioned visits, letters, phone calls, gifts, and other attentions that meant a lot to them. Almost three-fourths of the women and half the men saw a child at least weekly. Even when the children lived too far for frequent contact (or were no longer living), photographs on tables and walls in respondents' residences and memories of recent family gatherings served important emotional functions, according to the interviewers.

Those very old respondents who had no living children missed out on such services and relationships. Some gerontologists have suggested that more distant family members substitute for the absence of close kin, but this kind of substitution did not seem to be taking place in the USCF sample. By the time the respondents reached their present advanced age, most of their siblings and friends had died or were incapacitated or immobilized; nieces and nephews rarely filled the breach for the childless. While those oldest-old (married or not) with children seemed to have even more contact with other family members than with their children—96 percent of them who were still married and 89 percent of them who were widowed saw a family member (other than a child) weekly—only 30 percent of the unmarried childless reported seeing another family member weekly or more (Johnson and Troll, 1992). Perhaps children were a necessary link to the rest of the family.

What about grandchildren? Almost two-thirds of the old respondents (62%) reported they had both children and grandchildren living. This included 68 grandmothers and 25 grandfathers, almost three times as many grandmothers as grandfathers—gender differences that are unfortunate but meaningful. A large proportion (81%) of the grandmothers were rated as being very close to their grandchildren, but only about half of the men (53%) appeared close to a grandchild. In comparison with other data summarized above, there seemed a clear preference for children over grandchildren, at least at this time of life. It should be noted that grandchildren were important to many of the grandmothers, though only 35 percent of the sample were in contact with their grandchildren monthly or more often. The comparable rates for the grandfathers were lower but in the same direction. About half (60%) of the grandfathers reported they felt "close" to their child or children, and a quarter (28%) to a grandchild or grandchildren.

Suggested by these data is the pattern of children being pivotal links to others in the family. Reflecting this, almost all (93%) of the grandparents who were rated as close to a grandchild (or grandchildren) were also close to that child's (or those children's) parents. There was a significant correlation ($r = .34$) between expressive ties to children and those to grandchildren (Johnson and Troll, 1992). We can distinguish between the kind of closeness that is generic to all family members and the kind in which there is a particularistic link between two individuals. This is more likely to be true for grandchildren and other relatives than for children. In a few of the cases in the USCF sample, there was a particular direct connection between a grandparent and a grandchild. However, it appeared as if most of the relationships of the very old with their grandchildren could be considered "spillovers" from their closeness to their children. Further, particularistic relationships could exist with one grandchild and not with others—as it could with one child and not with others, as Aldous (1985) has noted in her research.

For example, one older woman in the USCF study said: "I have one daughter who is married. I talk to her every day and see her at least once a week. She has four boys. The youngest one lives here—on his own." (She meant that he actually lived in her house.) "He walked in bag and baggage. I was really enjoying my privacy. He moved in three years ago. He's 25. I asked my daughter if she kicked him out or something. She said no, he just decided he wanted to be on his own. I have another grandson in San Francisco, another in San Jose, and one in Louisiana. The one in the city (San Francisco) I see probably every two weeks. The one in San Jose is mad because he wanted to move in here and didn't. I told him I don't have anything to say about anything, anyway. Besides they had one child at the time and now they have two."

She was much more enthusiastic about the grandson who had moved to Louisiana than about the other three, who are in closer geographic proximity. This seemed like a true person-to-person attachment, like that with her daughter, while her relationship with the other three grandsons, including the one who lived in her house, did her shopping, and fixed things, seemed more generic. Her closest ties remain with her daughter, who seems more like a best friend than a child.

It should be mentioned that about the same percentage of "closeness" was seen for mother-daughter and for mother-son dyads—78 percent for each. There was also little difference between father-daughter (60%) and father-son (50%) dyads. It would not be surprising to find that the women's relationships were somewhat closer than the men's, given that most findings about gender differences note this effect.

Two-thirds (68%) of the 68 women in the USCF sample, and 84 percent of the 25 men who had both children and grandchildren, were seen at the second and third rounds of follow-up interviews, which were approximately 14 months apart. Half (59%) of the women and a quarter (29%) of the men reported being about as close to their children and grandchildren, after about four years of the study, as they had been at the first interview. And this was in the face of gradual deterioration in health and functioning. There was no significant difference in closeness at Time-1 between those for whom there are follow-ups and those who died or dropped out of the study for other reasons. About a quarter of the survivors—13 women and four men—reported more distant relationships at Time-2 or 3 than at Time-1, although in a few cases, a downturn at Time-2 reversed itself at Time-3. To the extent that generalizations can be made on the basis of such relatively few cases, it was the relationships with grandchildren that deteriorated or weakened, while those with children stayed more or less the same. A crucial question for consideration is this: Can we attribute this decline to withdrawal from less important relationships as the strength of the oldest-old family member weakens?

Those whose relationships got closer over time are perhaps more interesting than those who became less close, in view of the gender difference. While only 13 percent of the women got closer to their children or grandchildren, half of the men reported that they did. And it seems it was to their grandchildren that they got closer. Was it because the grandchildren—many in their 40s with children in their 20s—were older and freed of their own childrearing responsibilities that they could give thought and time to their grandparents? Or was it because the wives of the grandparents were weakening and opening space for attention from other family members? This attention from grandchildren was rarely direct help, it should be noted, but more like intermittent visiting, phone calls, and auxiliary service like shopping. One widower whose two granddaughters were in Europe and Southern California, respectively, had had a letter from the first and a weekend visit from the other just before the interview. It seemed apparent that these were particularistic relationships and very important to him.

WHAT DO OLD FAMILY MEMBERS DO FOR THEIR CHILDREN AND GRANDCHILDREN?

Since only the old people were interviewed in Johnson's USCF study, we need to look at the family analyses of the USC longitudinal study of three and four generations (Bengtson and Roberts, 1991) to determine the contribution of the very old to their families. Relatively few of the oldest generation members in the USC study, begun in 1991, are now as old as the San Francisco respondents, so we cannot make a direct comparison. The original USC sample consisted of over 350 three-generation families of adult members (the mean age of the grandchild generation was 19), 2,044 of whom returned questionnaires in the baseline 1971 survey (Bengtson, 1975). There have been four waves of survey data-collection in this study as well as extensive interviews with several subsamples of families.

Reported below are some results of interviews conducted by the study's first author with members of 10 extended families selected from the longitudinal study panel. These 10 families were selected because the first generation, the grandparents—what Hagestad (1985) calls the "omega generation"—had recently died; the original focus of inquiry concerned the effect of these deaths on the surviving family members. Their children and grandchildren, members of the second and third generations in these families, were interviewed in 1989 and 1990. The 10 families comprised more than 30 nuclear family units and more than 100 individuals, about half of whom were direct respondents of the original sample. The analyses involve case studies by family, following the model of Hess and Handel's (1959) *Family Worlds*. We looked at many aspects of the families, including the personality characteristics of the members and their dyadic relationships, as well as larger family indices such as who lived near whom, what their rituals were—for example, what holidays did they observe together, and how did they do so—and what their common beliefs and behaviors were ("consensual solidarity," in the Bengtson, Olander, and Haddad [1976] theoretical model).

One of the most obvious findings from these analyses was the importance of the grandparents, the oldest generation, for the families' integration. They had indeed served as "kin-keepers," and this was respected through the second and third generations of the study. The term "kin-keeper" has been used by a number of family researchers recently (e.g., Rosenthal, 1985) to denote those family members who spread the news, arrange get-togethers, and otherwise promote solidarity and unity among their kin.

The 10 families in this intensive case-study analysis show considerable variation in family organization. Some have maintained remarkably close-knit structures over time, with continued frequent communication that overrides distance, with a network of clearly defined kin-keepers, and with significant interaction rituals. By contrast, a few are characterized by what appears to be disengaged, almost disintegrated intergenerational structure, with minimal communication (just enough to know who is dead and who is alive and who lives where), with no defined roles, and with infrequent interactional rituals.

Nevertheless, it is noteworthy that even in the most fragmented of these families, there seem to be at least one or two individuals who try to keep the family together or attempt to build a new fabric from the shreds of the old relationships. It may be that this longitudinal sample was originally skewed toward family integration, since individuals in 1971 would not have been likely to participate in a study on families if they did not feel some connection with their relatives. Nevertheless, 20 years later, the case studies of these particular families indicate a high degree of individual interest in intergenerational connections, maintained at some expense in time, energy, and negotiation across generations and geographic distance.

One of our original hypotheses was that the death of the grandparents would lead to significant familial restructuring—and even the possible breakup of the intergenerational family kinship system. This did not seem to occur in these families. In those cases where the second-generation siblings (G-2s, children of the now-dead G-1 grandparents) did appear to have separated into divergent interactional branches, the brothers and sisters had not been close to each other for many years. In fact, it is plausible that the death of their parents brought as many siblings together as it tended to separate. There was occasional evidence of dismay over wills and distribution of property, but this seemed to cause permanent disruption in only one family, where it appeared to be the straw that broke the camel's back in terms of longstanding interactional problems. In the other nine families, some accommodation seemed to be made to resentments over time.

In eight of the 10 families, the "kin-keepers" were women, in each case the grandmother. When they died, the most common linkage was the G-2 family ties, usually cemented by the kin-keeping activities of a sister who had been "trained" by her mother to succeed her in kin-keeping. That is, when the grandmother had been functioning vigorously as the primary kin-keeper, her daughter had gradually helped her with more kin-keeping functions such as spreading the news and arranging periodic get-togethers. This assistantship appeared to increase over the years as the original kin-keeper became more feeble. Sometimes more than one sister, or two cousins, would be assistant kin-keepers to their mother or grandmother and remain as co-kin-keepers after her death. In one family, co-kin-keepers were sisters-in-law. Since all the grandparental deaths were fairly recent—the oldest took place eight years before the interviews—it could be that such co-kin-keepers would eventually head separate branches of their own.

To give an example: The "Berger" family appeared to be the most integrated of the 10, perhaps partly because it has fewer members and only granddaughters. When the only daughter, Bonnie, married her second husband and "grew up" (her first marriage had been when she was a pregnant high school student), she moved to Northern California, leaving her parents and brother in Los Angeles. From that time on, her mother, Ada, enlarged the scope of her kin-keeping to include visits to San Francisco every few months. When the grandfather died, Ada began to live half the year with Bonnie in San Francisco and half with her divorced son, Boris, in her old house in Los Angeles. She arranged family get-togethers to include everybody from both cities at least several times a year. By 1988, Ada was blind, and her arthritis made it difficult for her to manage stairs or other activities. She drew back in her role of kin-keeper as Bonnie gradually took over bringing them all together—there were now two children in the fourth generation. Bonnie's daughter Hester was in the process of becoming Bonnie's assistant in kin-keeping when Ada died.

An example of an opposite pattern, one of kin disengagement and near disintegration, can be seen in the "Caldwell" family, in which the grandfather, Adam, was an Army regular. Adam and his first wife, the mother of his two daughters, each married several times. Adam was transferred from one part of the country to another during his Army career (he was originally from Alabama), but when he retired from the service and became a civilian technician, he settled in California with his current wife and her children (his stepchildren), not too far from where his older daughter, Carrie, lived with her second husband and his (not her) children—her children lived with their father, her first husband. To the extent that there was any kin-keeping in this family, it was done by grandfather Adam. Carrie and her sister Nora, who lives on the East Coast, have had minimal contact since they reached adulthood, but until just before Adam's death (the grandmother died earlier) he spent his vacations visiting his children and grandchildren.

Carrie is almost as distant from her two children as she is from her sister. Her daughter moved to Hawaii and her son to South Africa. Her sister Nora, who has six children, has been in and out of marriages and mental hospitals most of her adult life. Nora's oldest son, Stuart, who had been a drug addict living "on the street" during most of his youth, eventually joined a rehabilitation clinic, where he now works and tries to save others, including his mother and half-siblings. His contacts with his grandfather Adam were very meaningful to him, and he now seems to be taking over Adam's kin-keeping activities.

As noted above, eight of the 10 families had female kin-keepers; only two had men, Adam and a teacher who emigrated from Costa Rica with his family when his four daughters reached adulthood. Most of the grandmothers were more or less like Ada, vigorously keeping their children and grandchildren (and sometimes siblings and in-laws) together as long as they were physically able, and handing down the kin-keeping role to daughters and granddaughters when they got too old.

If we compare these grandparental kin-keepers with the over-85 respondents in the USCF study, we may be able to trace a trajectory, for very few of the oldest-old were still active kin-keepers. Part of what the oldest family members give to their families is the memory of what they did for them and the model of how the next generations can carry on the pattern. Much of the significance of the family for the oldest-old is the *gestalt* of meanings symbolized in memories and expressive services. Their contribution to the young is perhaps also more symbolic than instrumental, although it should be mentioned that most of the now-dead grandparents were deeply mourned.

CONCLUSIONS

The data summarized above from two empirical studies concerning family relations of the oldest-old suggest three conclusions. First, intergenerational relationships do contribute to the adaptation of individuals in late-late life, and those who do not have children and grandchildren to provide solidarity and support are very much disadvantaged as they negotiate the hazards of advanced old age. Second, the old-old do contribute to the family, well into the last stages of life, as kin-keepers and enhancers of family solidarity. When they die, their roles tend to be taken on by younger family members, particularly daughters. Third—and this is perhaps most important—we note that the family relations of the oldest-old must be considered in a life-course, intergenerational context of giving and receiving, solidarity and negotiation—and that much more research is necessary before we can begin to appreciate the complex ways in which family relations mitigate the many problems of aging.

* * *

Lillian E. Troll, Ph.D., is professor emeritus, Department of Psychology, Rutgers University, and adjunct professor of human development and aging and anthropology, University of California, San Francisco. Vern L. Bengtson, Ph.D., is professor, Division of Social and Behavioral Science, University of Southern California, Los Angeles.

REFERENCES

Aldous, J., 1985. "Parent–Adult Child Relations as Affected by the Grandparent Status." In V. L. Bengtson and J. F. Robertson, eds., *Grandparenthood*. Beverly Hills, Calif.: Sage, pp. 117–32.

Archbold, P. G., 1982. All-Consuming Activity: The Family as Caregiver. *Generations* 7(2): 12–13.

Bengtson, V. L., 1975. "Generation and Family Effects in Value Socialization." *American Sociological Review* 40: 358–71.

Bengtson, V. L. and Roberts, R.E.L., 1991. "Intergenerational Solidarity in Aging Families: An Example of Formal Theory Construction." *Journal of Marriage and the Family* 53:856–70.

Bengtson, V. L., Rosenthal, C. J. and Burton, L. M., 1990. "Families and Aging: Diversity and Heterogeneity." In R. Binstock and L. George, eds., *Handbook of Aging and the Social Sciences*, 3d ed. New York: Academic Press. pp. 263–87.

Bengtson, V. L., Olander, E. B. and Haddad, E. A., 1976. "The 'Generation Gap' and Aging Family Members: Toward a Conceptual Model." In J. E. Gubrium, ed., *Time, Roles, and Self in Old Age*. New York: Human Sciences Press, pp. 237–63.

Gatz, M., Bengtson, V. L. and Blum, M., 1990. "Caregiving Families." In J. E. Birren and K. W. Schaie, eds., *Handbook of the Psychology of Aging*, 3d ed., San Diego: Academic Press, pp. 404–26.

Hagestad, G. O., 1985. "Continuity and Connectedness." In V. L. Bengtson and J. F. Robertson, eds., *Grandparenthood*. Beverly Hills, Calif.: Sage, pp. 31–48.

Hess, R. and Handel, G.,1959. *Family Worlds: A Pychological Approach to Family Life*. Chicago: University of Chicago Press.

Johnson, C. L. and Troll, L., 1992. "Family Functioning in Late Late Life." *Journal of Gerontology, Social Sciences* 47: S66–S72.

Litwak, E., 1960. "Geographic Mobility and Extended Family Cohesion." *American Sociological Review* 25:9–21.

Rosenthal, C. J., 1985. "Kinkeeping in the Familial Division of Labor." *Journal of Marriage and the Family* 47:965–74.

Troll, L. E., 1991. "From Children to Grandchildren." Paper presented at the annual scientific meetings of the Gerontological Society of America, San Francisco, Nov. 22.

Troll, L. E., ed., 1986. *Family Issues in Current Gerontology*. New York: Springer.

Chapter 11

From Generation Unto Generation: Parent-Child Support in Aging American Families*

David J. Eggebeen

One of the fastest growing, and most exciting, areas of research on families is that of intergenerational exchanges of support. It is difficult not to find at least one article concerned with intergenerational topics in any recent issues of family, aging, or gerontological scholarly journals. Recent years have seen publication of a spate of books, convening of special conferences focused on intergenerational concerns, and sponsorship of data collection efforts featuring measures of intergenerational processes. Why are social scientists interested in intergenerational issues? What are we learning about contemporary generational relations in America today, and what might these findings tell us about the future? This chapter describes findings about patterns of intergenerational exchanges of support in contemporary American families from one survey, the National Survey of Families and Households. This survey, to be described more fully below, has had a major impact on scholarship on the family since its release in late 1988. Before

*Support for this research was provided by NICHD Grant No. 1 RO1 HD26070 "Intergenerational Exchanges in Families with Children," Dennis P. Hogan, Principal Investigator, and by the Population Research Institute's NICHD Population Center Grant. Funds for the computer analysis were provided by the Pennsylvania State University Intercollege Research Programs.

discussing what we can learn about aging-parent/adult-child ties from these data, however, it is useful to review the reasons for the mounting interest, among scholars and policy makers, in intergenerational exchanges of support.

WHY THE RECENT INTEREST IN INTERGENERATIONAL EXCHANGES?

The reasons for the burst of scholarly activity in intergenerational exchanges of support are several. For starters, it is hard to ignore the ongoing changes in the American family. Most of these are well known: The formation of new nuclear families has slowed as the age of marriage has climbed. A growing proportion of men and women do not marry at all, and among those who do, a large proportion begin their unions with a period of cohabitation. Patterns of childbearing have changed markedly in the past few decades. Having babies is increasingly being postponed by some women, while among others, having children outside of marriage is becoming more common. Increases in separation and divorce have reduced the perceived permanence of marriage, while remarriage has led to more complex "blended" family structures. Finally, the post–World War II years have been marked by a "subtle revolution" in women's roles; especially significant have been the large increases in the number of married women with children entering or staying in the labor force (Bumpass, 1990; Furstenberg et al., 1983; Hogan, 1987; Modell, 1989; Rindfuss, Morgan and Swicegood, 1989).

Scholars from a wide range of disciplines, perspectives, and interests have been busy for some time identifying these changes, speculating about their origins, and assessing their consequences. While the implications of these shifts for intergenerational ties have been a major focus, most of the attention has been on the parent-child relationships when children are still small. Only recently have gerontologists, and others with interests in aging, begun to follow through on the logic of a life-course perspective and ask what the effects of these social changes might be for parent-child ties in the later life course.

Social changes other than those occurring in families have heightened interest in intergenerational processes. Structural changes in the economy in the past two decades have eroded the ability of families to be economically self-sufficient. The average earnings for males, especially those without a college education, have fallen in the 1980s (Levy and Michel, 1991). But for the shift from the single male breadwinner model of the 1950s and 1960s to the "two earner" model predominant in the 1980s, family incomes would have declined (Bianchi and Spaine, 1986). Even with this compensatory change, growth in family incomes has remained essentially flat since the mid-1970s. The ability of families to survive economically has been further exacerbated by the fact that an increasingly larger percentage of them are single-parent families—by definition dependent on one income.

Clearly, trends in government spending on family and child-oriented programs over the 1980s would not lead one to conclude that the state has stepped into the breach. Both the budgeted amounts and the political rhetoric suggest a shift toward seeing families, rather than the state, as best at "taking care of their needy" (Select Committee on Children, Youth, and Families, 1988; Weinraub 1981). These social, economic, and political changes raise questions about how families are making ends meet. To what extent, for example, are families embedded in support networks that assist them in times of financial need? How good a job are families doing at taking care of their needy members?

Finally, changes in life expectancy have dramatically increased the number of multigenerational families and the number of years that any individual can expect to be part of a multigenerational family situation (see article by Christine Himes, Chapter 3). For the first time in human history, significant proportions of individuals are surviving into middle age with one or both parents still alive. Not surprisingly, academic and popular interest in the nature of parent-child ties in the later life course has been spurred at least partly because of these demographic shifts.

It is in the context of these events that interest in kinship ties has rekindled among scholars and policy analysts. More than ever, recognition has grown that even in advanced societies, kin play a strategic role in assisting families and individuals in need over the entire life course. Just how dependent are families today on assistance from kin? Is it safe to assume that most individuals can depend on their parents or adult children for help when in need? Are some groups more "familial" than others? We turn to the National Survey of Families and Households to address these issues.

THE NATIONAL SURVEY OF FAMILIES AND HOUSEHOLDS

The National Survey of Families and Households (NSFH) is a nationally representative survey of 13,017 respondents interviewed in 1987–88. Personal interviews and supplemental questionnaires were employed to gather a rich set of data on the past and current family relationships of the respondents. The impact of these data on family scholarship has been profound. In the short time it has been available to the scholarly public (it was released to researchers in late 1988), it has become one of the most popular secondary-data sources for empirical research. Much of what we are learning about American families in the late 1980s has or will come from scholarship using these data. The reasons for this popularity are several. The survey is sufficiently large to ensure adequate analysis of interesting subpopulations—for example, widowed elderly, black single parents, cohabitating couples. It contains a broad array of questions covering most of the significant domains of interest to family scholars: marital, fertility, and work histories; household structure; questions on sexual behavior, domestic labor, physical and mental health; family background; and information on children, for example. And, most important for our interests, extensive questions probe social network ties, kin relations, and material and psychic exchanges—the survey contains a variety of indicators of the extent to which family behavior extends across households.

Intergenerational support is assessed in several different ways in these data (e.g., quality of relationships, frequency of contact, whom one would ask for emergency assistance, receipt of home mortgage assistance or inheritances), and for a variety of individuals (brothers and sisters, parents, adult children, other relatives, friends). But we will limit our discussion to the questions on whether the respondent gave or received various types of aid in the past month (money, household assistance, childcare or care during illness, and emotional support or advice), since they are most relevant to gauging the extent of "routine" intergenerational flows of assistance. Furthermore, we focus on one "stem" in the network of individuals on whom respondents potentially draw (and to whom they provide support)—the parent-child relationship. For most individuals, this relationship remains their most salient kin tie through their life course (Rossi and Rossi, 1990).

In the analysis of these data, we have approached intergenerational exchanges in a number of different ways. We have documented the flows of support from the perspective of adult children and assessed the extent to which exchanges of specific items might be linked (Eggebeen and Hogan, 1990; Hogan, Eggebeen and Clogg, 1992). We have also examined exchange patterns from the perspective of aging parents (Eggebeen, 1991). Specific attention has been given to sources of assistance in old age (Hogan and Eggebeen, 1991a), those aging parents "in the middle" (Hogan and Eggebeen, 1991b), and the well-being of individuals with extremely old parents (Hogan, Eggebeen and Snaith, 1991). What follows represents some (but not all) of the major themes of our work cited here. We begin by describing overall patterns of exchanges. This is followed by a discussion of the extent to which support flows are responsive to variations in family structure. Finally, we conclude with an examination of race and ethnic differences in the observed patterns of support exchanged.

ROUTINE ASSISTANCE IN AMERICAN FAMILIES

One of the most striking findings in the analyses of these data is that routine exchanges between generations are not all that common. Looking first from the perspective of adult children, we find that only 17 percent received money (at least $200 given or loaned in the past 5 years) from their parents and only 4 percent gave money. In the past month before the interview, only about 13 percent of adult children received childcare, 17 percent received household assistance, and 32 percent gave household assistance. Advice and emotional support are the most common forms of exchange, with 27 percent of these respondents receiving such support and another 25 percent giving such support to their parents (Eggebeen and Hogan, 1990).

Since it is likely that various types of assistance rendered or received go together, a latent structure analysis was performed on the combination of giving and receiving on each of the four dimensions. This analysis suggests that patterns of intergenerational exchanges can be characterized by four types: persons not involved in any exchanges, persons who give only advice, persons who only receive assistance, and persons highly involved in giving and receiving support. Over half of all adult children (who themselves are parents of dependent children) are uninvolved in exchanges with their parents. Nineteen percent are "receivers only" of assistance, 17 percent are advice givers, and only 11 percent are enmeshed in strong exchange networks (i.e, "high" exchangers) (Hogan, Eggebeen and Clogg, 1992).

The picture is much the same from the perspective of aging parents. Parents aged 55 and older with at least one adult child living independently report comparatively higher levels of assistance given and received from their adult children than was the case when we examined exchanges from the perspective of adult children. This is to be expected, of course, given that children typically have only one set of parents with whom to engage in exchanges, while most aging parents can potentially draw support from several children. In spite of this theoretically greater opportunity for support, the levels of exchange reported are still modest. Giving advice is the most frequent exchange (42%), followed by giving money (33%) and receiving advice and giving childcare (both 29%), but they are all typical of well under half of these respondents. Only one in five aging parents have received assistance with household chores, transportation, or household repairs from any of their adult children in the past month. Receiving monetary assistance is virtually unheard of (3%). At any given point in time, more than one-third of the elderly are not involved in giving and over 60 percent have not received anything from any of their adult children (Eggebeen, 1991).

Perhaps the problem is that these "averages" hide significant variations in assistance by such factors as the quality of the relationships between parents and children, the levels of contact (visits, phone calls, letters), and the distance they live apart. To address this issue, we examined the levels of exchange for those families characterized by parents and at least one adult child living within 10 miles of each other, having contact at least once a week, and reporting their relationship as good or excellent. In general, close-knit families are significantly more likely to be exchanging support. Even among these families, however, more than a third report no involvement in exchanges, and only 26 percent could be characterized as "high" exchangers (Hogan, Eggebeen and Clogg, 1992).

THE ROLE OF FAMILY STRUCTURE
IN EXCHANGES BETWEEN GENERATIONS

One of the most important sources of variation in exchange patterns is family structure. From the perspective of the adult child, the more siblings one has, the less likely it is that one is receiving support from parents. Aging parents are less able to help any individual child when they have had more children, indicating that the trade-off between number of children and the degree of assistance persists even into the later years of family life (Blake, 1989). There does not, however, appear to be much "free riding" on the part of these adult children—levels of giving support to parents are not affected by number of siblings. From the perspective of aging parents, then, having a large number of children "pays off" in later life, as the likelihood of receiving assistance increases with each additional adult child (Eggebeen, 1991; Eggebeen and Hogan, 1990; Hogan, Eggebeen and Clogg, 1992).

Grandchildren, especially preschool-aged children, are a key factor in getting support from aging parents (grandparents). Grandparents frequently take an active role in the lives of their children by providing childcare and household assistance at a time when parents need help (Eggebeen and Hogan, 1990).

Intergenerational support varies by the marital situations of both adult children and aging parents. Married adult children tend to give more assistance to their parents than do their nonmarried counterparts, while the unmarried tend to receive more help. Aging parents less often provide assistance to stepchildren, but the parents' likelihood of receiving aid is unaffected by this relationship. Widowed aging parents elicit higher levels of support from adult children than do married parents, although this support is not automatic—those who are in good health and socioeconomically secure do not receive much additional support (Eggebeen and Hogan, 1990; Eggebeen, 1991).

Increases in longevity have raised the likelihood of middle-aged Americans experiencing a multigenerational family situation. Still, it is less common than one might presuppose, given the media attention to this topic. As of 1988, only about one in four adults are "in the middle" generationally, that is, simultaneously have at least one adult child aged 19 or older and a living parent aged 65 or older. Of course, this situation varies significantly by age—over 40 percent of adults between the ages of 45 and 54 are experiencing this situation. Is this a burdensome position? The data suggest not. Only about one-fifth of these individuals in the middle generation have parents whom they characterize as being in poor health. Yet even among these, only a third are actually giving some form of assistance to the parent (Hogan and Eggebeen, 1991b).

RACE AND ETHNIC VARIATIONS IN SUPPORT

Race and ethnic differences in the incidence of intergenerational support evident in these data stand in stark contrast to the portrait of family ties among minority groups depicted in past research (e.g., Bastida 1979; Markides, Boldt and Ray, 1986; Stack, 1974; Taylor, 1986, 1988; Wilson, 1986). There is little evidence that Mexican Americans reflect higher levels of social support exchanged between generations. Certainly the migration experience of a substantial proportion of this ethnic group creates a serious barrier to intergenerational support. However, even when physical distance between the generations is taken into account, there is no greater level of exchange among Mexican American families compared to families of the majority population (Eggebeen and Hogan, 1990; Hogan, Eggebeen and Clogg, 1992).

African Americans are consistently less likely than whites or Mexican Americans to be involved in any sort of intergenerational assistance (Eggebeen and Hogan, 1990; Hogan, Eggebeen and Clogg, 1992). Even when socioeconomic resources (income, education), personal characteristics (gender, age, marital status, health status), and characteristics of parents (health status, levels of education) are taken into account, black Americans remain only 48 percent as likely as whites to be high exchangers, only 67 percent as likely as whites to receive support from their parents, and only 57 percent as likely to give advice to their parents (Hogan, Eggebeen and Clogg, 1992). These findings are consistent with recent ethnographic work which suggests that multigenerational black families in need often lack the financial and human capital resources to meet the needs of all generations adequately (Burton, 1991).

How can we understand these findings, given the portrait presented by research done in the 1970s of black families having exceptionally strong and effective kin support networks? There is growing consensus that the plight of black Americans worsened in the 1980s. The erosion of neighborhoods and communities within cities, the declining employment prospects of young black males, and the accelerating changes in family structure (relative to whites) mean that increasing numbers of black families are being placed in situations in which the demands on them are large, and their capacity to offer effective assistance is limited (Wilson, 1987). Perhaps these data point to how much has changed among black families in the past decade more than they correct erroneous characterizations drawn from past ethnographic work.

CONCLUSIONS

During the 1980s Americans were in frequent contact with their noncoresident parents or adult children. They also tended, on average, to rate these intergenerational relationships very positively. Frequent contacts and good relations, however, are not characterized by high levels of regular exchange. Although American parents do not typically engage in exchanges with their adult children in the absence of pressing needs, these data suggest that when needs arise, support networks are mobilized and assistance is forthcoming.

This is not to say, however, that these observed patterns of low levels of exchange are not cause for concern. There is some suggestion that the kinds and sources of assistance one draws on in a crisis are at least partly determined by a history of routine exchanges between the individual in need and the provider (Hogan and Eggebeen, 1991a). Furthermore, the amounts and types of support depend on the resource levels of each generation and the competing demands for their support. For some, this means that family support is absent during times of need. Family support clearly helps, but for many, family exchanges alone are inadequate to deal with problems of teenage pregnancy, poverty, single parenthood, widowhood, disability, or poor health.

*   *   *

David J. Eggebeen, Ph.D., is assistant professor of human development and research associate, Population Research Institute, Pennsylvania State University, University Park.

REFERENCES

Bastida, E., 1979. "Family Integration in Later Life Among Hispanic Americans." *Journal of Minority Aging* 4:42–49.

Bianchi, S. and Spaine, D., 1986. *American Women in Transition.* New York: Russell Sage Foundation.

Blake, J., 1989. *Family Size and Achievement.* Berkeley: University of California Press.

Bumpass, L. L., 1990. "What's Happening to the American Family? Interactions Between Demographic and Institutional Change." *Demography* 27:483–98.

Burton, L. M., 1991. "Survival, Resilience, and Vulnerability in the Life Course of Black Families: A Multigenerational Perspective." Paper presented at the conference "Fostering Resilience," Institute for Mental Health Initiatives and the National Institute of Mental Health, Washington, D.C.

Eggebeen, D. J., 1991. "Family Structure and Intergenerational Exchanges." Paper presented at the annual meeting of the Population Association of America, March.

Eggebeen, D. J. and Hogan, D. P., 1990. "Giving Between the Generations in American Families." *Human Nature* 1:211–32.

Furstenberg, F. F. et al., 1983. "The Life Course of Children of Divorce: Marital Disruption and Parental Contact." *American Sociological Review* 48:656–68.

Hogan, D. P., 1987. "Demographic Trends in Human Fertility and Parenting Across the Lifespan." In J. B. Lancaster et al., eds., *Parenting Across the Lifespan: Biosocial Dimensions*. New York: Aldine.

Hogan, D. P. and Eggebeen, D. J., 1991a. "Sources of Aid and Assistance in Old Age." Paper presented at the annual meeting of the American Sociological Association, August.

Hogan, D. P. and Eggebeen, D. J., 1991b. "American Adults in the Middle: Patterns of Giving and Receiving Between the Generations." Paper presented at the annual meeting of the Gerontological Society of America, November.

Hogan, D. P., Eggebeen, D. J. and Snaith, S., 1991. "The Well-Being of Aging Americans with Very Old Parents." Paper presented at the Delaware Conference on Intergenerational Relations. University of Delaware, October.

Hogan, D. P., Eggebeen, D. J. and Clogg, C. C., 1992. "The Structure of Intergenerational Exchanges in American Families." Unpublished manuscript, Population Research Institute, Pennsylvania State University.

Levy, F. and Michel, R. C., 1991. *The Economic Future of American Families: Income and Wealth Trends*. Washington, D.C.: Urban Institute.

Markides, K. S., Boldt, J. S. and Ray, L. A., 1986. "Sources of Helping and Intergenerational Relations." *Journal of Gerontology* 41: 506–11.

Modell, J., 1989. *Into One's Own: From Youth to Adulthood in the United States, 1920–1975*. Berkeley: University of California Press.

Rindfuss, R., Morgan, S. P. and Swicegood, G., 1989. *First Births in America: Changes in the Timing of Parenthood*. Berkeley: University of California Press.

Rossi, A. S. and Rossi, P. H., 1990. *Of Human Bonding: Parent-Child Relations Across the Life Course*. New York: Aldine De Gruyter.

Select Committee on Children, Youth and Families, 1988. "U.S. Children and Their Families: Current Conditions and Recent Trends, 1989." Washington, D.C.: Government Printing Office.

Stack, C., 1974. *All Our Kin: Strategies for Survival in the Black Community*. New York: Harper & Row.

Taylor, R. J., 1986. "Receipt of Support from Family Among Black Americans: Demographic and Familial Differences," *Journal of Marriage and the Family* 48:67–77.

Taylor, R. J., 1988. "Aging and Supportive Relationships Among Black Americans." In J. Jackson, ed., *The Black American Family*. New York: Springer.

Wilson. M., 1986. "The Black Extended Family: An Analytical Consideration." *Developmental Psychology* 22: 246–58.

Wilson, W. J., 1987. *The Truly Disadvantaged*. Chicago: University of Chicago Press.

Weinraub, B., 1981. "Home Care Is Pushed in Senate as Alternative to Institutions for the Aged." *New York Times*, 16 April.

Chapter 12

Challenges and Rewards: African American Grandparents as Surrogate Parents*

Linda Burton and Cynthia deVries

African American grandparents, particularly grandmothers, have historically played a pivotal role in African American families (Frazier, 1939; Huling, 1978; White, 1985). For example, in her recent anthology of poems, Maya Angelou (1990) salutes the strengths of and challenges to African American grandmothers, whom she describes as follows:

> These momma faces, lemon-yellow, plum-purple,
> honey-brown, have grimaced and twisted
> down a pyramid of years.
> She is Sheba and Sojourner,
>   Harriet and Zora,
>   Mary Bethune and Angela,
>   Annie to Zenobia.

> She stands
> before the abortion clinic,
> confounded by the lack of choices.

*The research described in this chapter was supported by grants to the first author from the Brookdale Foundation, William T. Grant Foundation, and the National Institute of Mental Health (No. R29MH46057-01).

In the Welfare line,
reduced to the pity of handouts.
Ordained in the pulpit, shielded
by the mysteries.
In the operating room,
husbanding life.
In the choir loft,
holding God in her throat.
On lonely street corners,
hawking her body.
In the classroom, loving the
children to understanding.

Centered on the world's stage,
she sings to her loves and beloveds,
to her foes and detractors:
However I am perceived and deceived,
however my ignorance and conceits,
lay aside your fears that I will be undone,

for I shall not be moved.

This brief excerpt from Maya Angelou's work touches upon two themes that continue to emerge in the family lives of some contemporary African American grandparents—surrogate parenting and survival of the family (Scott, 1991). For example, given the current increases in parental joblessness, poverty, and single parenthood in African American families, grandparents are often called upon to assume the role of surrogate parent to their grandchildren (Burton and Dilworth-Anderson, 1991; Apfel and Seitz, 1991; Farley and Allen, 1987; Tinsley and Parke, 1984). For many elderly African American men and women, assumption of this role requires a long-term commitment to provide care and support for their grandchildren. Many of these grandparents, like their predecessors, view their role as a mechanism for family survival. Yet, most grandparents note that while the role of surrogate parent has its rewards, it can also be quite challenging. The purpose of this chapter is to briefly describe the challenges and rewards experienced by African American grandparents who are rearing their grandchildren. We have chosen to do this by using the voices of 101 grandparents and great-grandparents involved in two of our ethnographic studies.

Study 1 was conducted in a Northwestern urban community from December 1988 to June 1989 and involved 15 African American women age 43–70. These grandmothers and great-grandmothers were recruited through a grandmother's support group and through referrals from a local family-service agency. Five of the respondents were employed at the time of the study; three were on leave of absence from their jobs; four were receiving welfare; and three identified themselves as retired. Eight of the women were currently married; two were divorced; two were separated; and three were widowed. Eleven of the women were grandmothers and four were great-grandmothers. The number of children being raised by the respondents ranged from two to five, and the ages of the children from 2 months to 13 years.

Respondents in Study 2 included grandmothers, great-grandmothers, and grandfathers. This study, which is ongoing, is currently being conducted in a Northeastern urban community. Respondents were recruited through referrals from black churches and social service agencies, and by networking with community residents. The purpose of this study is to examine the effects of teenage childbearing on the family roles of older women and men. To date, 42 grandmothers, age 29–69; 25 great-grandmothers, age 51–82; and 19 grandfathers, age 62–78, have been interviewed. Although the sample is still developing, we anticipate that the ranges for socioeconomic and marital statuses of the respondents will be comparable. The interviews conducted with the respondents have lasted anywhere from three hours to seven hours. As did the grandparents in Study 1, these men and women also shared their life stories with us, highlighting what they see as the challenges and rewards they currently experience in their role as surrogate parents to their grandchildren.

THE CHALLENGES OF SURROGATE PARENTING

Our grandparents identified several challenges for us. First, the majority of our grandparents talked about those they face in providing care for multiple generations. Many of our grandparents and great-grandparents were not only taking care of their grandchildren but their adult children and frail elderly relatives as well. One great-grandmother, whom we shall call Sarah, shared her story with us. Sarah is 63 years old. Currently, Sarah's 35-year-old daughter with four children of her own, plus three of her brother's children, live with Sarah. Two of Sarah's teenage granddaughters are pregnant—one is expecting her first child; the other, her second. In addition to providing a place to live, food to eat, and childcare for the family members who live with her, Sarah also travels back and forth to a nearby state to help another adult daughter, who is going through a divorce, and another granddaughter, who has recently had a child.

"Can you believe that I do all this?" Sarah said. "I can't even believe it myself. All these people depend on me. I am stretched so thin that sometimes I wonder if I can seriously make it. I guess that I have no choice. Look at how old I look. I bet you thought that I was about 80, didn't you? Most people think I am."

Pervis, a 62-year-old grandfather, expressed his feelings this way:

> "I got a lot on my back. I take care of my wife who has cancer and my two grandbabies. Sometimes, I think that it's a losing battle. But I have faith in the Almighty and I have two good boys who help me. They aren't able to be here all the time because they have families too. You can't ask for more than that."

The situation of yet another family in our current study aptly demonstrates the range of challenges for providing care for multiple generations. Mavis, age 65, is a grandmother of four, mother of three, and works part time at minimum wage for a janitorial service. With her limited salary she provided a home, utilities, and food for her household. In late February she lost her rental home because past due payments had not been made. Mavis moved her family into her sister's home rather than obtaining housing at a local shelter for the homeless.

In March, Mavis became a grandmother for yet another time. Her youngest daughter, who turned 14 just prior to the birth, did not have the financial support of her child's father. There were no provisions set aside for the myriad items that a newborn infant needs. When Mavis was interviewed prior to the birth of her grandchild and we asked what feelings she had about the role of grandparent, she responded, "I don't have time to think about that stuff. I have too much to do." One of the things she had to do was find affordable housing for her growing family.

A second challenge noted by the grandparents involved providing care for their grandchildren. Most of the grandparents acknowledged the fact that they deeply loved and were committed to their grandchildren and that, at times, their role was personally very gratifying. However, several grandparents indicated that there were "just so many things they had to deal with" in providing care for their grandchildren.

Two special concerns were voiced by the grandparents with respect to their childcare responsibilities. The first reflects what the grandparents discussed as "long-term and permanent" surrogate parenting. Ida, an 82-year-old great-grandmother expressed her feelings this way:

> "I had my great-grandbaby since she was 2 years old. Now she is 15. That's a long time to have somebody's child. I guess she will be with me till I die."

Simon, a 67-year-old grandfather, commented further:

> "I've had all three of my grandchildren since they were born. The oldest one is now 13 and the youngest 7. I had no idea I would be raising these children this long ... but their parents are in no shape to raise them right. I am going to be raising kids all my life, I just know it. I just know it."

The second concern involves the grandparents' ability to keep up with the school, social, and physical activities of their grandchildren. For example, Gloria, a 75-year-old great-grandmother, described her frustration with her grandson wanting her to take him to a local amusement park:

> "Can you just see me out there trying to get on a roller coaster at my age. I'm going to have to hire someone younger than me to take him there so he can have some fun."

Harold, a 68-year-old grandfather, commented on the frustration he felt in helping his granddaughter with her math homework:

> "I don't know nothing about this new arithmetic. I can't help her at all. I am too embarrassed to go to her teacher and tell her that I can't help. What can I do? I want her to make it."

Finally, all the respondents indicated that handling the myriad responsibilities of caregiving and surrogate parenting took a tremendous toll on their personal lives. Those respondents who were employed complained of the stress they felt in trying to accomplish all the "things they had to do." Three of the grandmothers in Study 1 took a leave of absence from their job to manage their caregiving responsibilities. It is not uncommon for the grandmothers in our current study to assume the parenting role within days of their grandchild's birth. Often they assume that role to the exclusion of their own social needs. A 62-year-old great-grandmother commented on the issue:

"I had to leave my job to take care of these babies. I gave up my seniority and my pension. I don't understand that, though. I'm trying to start a business out of my house so I can make some money. I have to do something with my hands. That makes me feel important."

Additionally, the grandparents reported that they had no time for themselves. Sheila, a 42-year-old grandmother, remarked:

"Sometimes I just would like to go off by myself, walk around the mall, buy a new dress. I can't do that now because the kids come first. As much as I want to, I can't."

Sheila's comments represent the struggle articulated by a number of the respondents. It was clear that the grandparents interviewed "loved their grandchildren to distraction" and were committed to taking care of them. The grandparents, however, had their own personal needs, which they felt they did not have the "freedom" to attend to. Many of the grandparents expressed feelings of guilt and shame about "wanting to do things for themselves when the children needed them so much." One great-grandmother commented:

"I wasn't raised to think about doing for myself. My grandmother taught me that I should think about what my family needs more than anything. I feel so bad sometimes because I need to do something for myself. I can't, though. These children need me."

THE REWARDS OF SURROGATE PARENTING

While many of the grandparents indicated that the surrogate parenting role was often challenging, they also stated that the role had its rewards. One of the rewards that a few of the grandparents described concerned the opportunity to parent again and, most important, this time to do it right. Rochelle, a 35-year-old grandmother, stated the following:

"I didn't do such a good job with my daughter, but this time I have the chance to do it right. I am going to be the best parent possible to my grandson. This time I have a chance to redeem myself."

Other grandparents noted that being responsible for their grandchildren afforded them the opportunity to nurture a legacy. One 65-year-old grandfather expressed that sentiment:

"I feel blessed that I can see our family line being carried down through my grandchildren. I'm going to invest all I can in them because our name needs to go on and our belief in God has to be carried forth."

Still other grandparents told us that the rewards that their grandchildren provided for them were companionship and love. One 80-year-old great-grandmother said:

"I don't know what I would do without my granddaughter. She is my best friend. With her here with me, even though she did have a baby, I feel like I will never be alone."

Estelle, a 52-year-old grandmother of a 14-year-old pregnant teen and three boys age 1, 2, and 5, noted further:

"I have been diagnosed with cancer three times. I'm on chemotherapy now. Do you know that raising these kids and receiving their love is what keeps me alive. Believe it! I'm not going anywhere until they are grown and have their own families. By then I'll be raising another group of kids. It will be my third time around. I thank God for the chance."

CONCLUSION

In this chapter we have briefly highlighted the challenges and rewards that a number of African American grandparents have experienced in raising their grandchildren. The comments of the grandparents presented here not only represent the 101 African American men and women interviewed in our studies, but quite possibly reflect the feelings of grandparents from a variety of ethnic/racial and socioeconomic groups who have also assumed a surrogate parent role for their grandchildren (Chescheir, 1981). As indicated by other chapters in this volume, family life and needs are changing rapidly given the current "demographic revolution" and political and economic agendas of American society. It appears that grandparents are being recruited by families and social services to address the needs of children whose parents are unable to care for them. The emerging question, however, is, Who will take care of the grandparents when they can no longer take care of themselves or their grandchildren? Although surrogate parenting has its rewards, it also poses serious challenges. Will we as a society create support for grandparents so that they can survive the challenges?

*　　*　　*

Linda Burton, Ph.D., is an associate professor, and Cynthia deVries is a graduate student, both in the Department of Human Development and Family Studies, Pennsylvania State University, University Park.

REFERENCES

Angelou, M., 1990. *I Shall Not Be Moved*. New York: Random House.

Apfel, N. H. and Seitz, V., 1991. "Four Models of Adolescent Mother–Grandmother Relationships in Black Inner-City Families." *Family Relations* 40(4):421–29.

Burton, L. M. and Dilworth-Anderson, P., 1991. "The Intergenerational Family Roles of Aged Black Americans." *Marriage and Family Review* 16 (3/4): 311–30.

Chescheir, M. W., 1981. "The Use of the Elderly as Surrogate Parents: A Clinical Perspective." *Journal of Gerontological Social Work* 3(1):3–15.

Farley, R. and Allen, W., 1987. *The Color Line and the Quality of Life in America*. New York: Russell Sage Foundation.

Frazier, E. F., 1939. *The Negro Family in the United States*. Chicago: University of Chicago Press.

Huling, W. E., 1978. "Evolving Family Roles for the Black Elderly." *Aging* 287:21–27.

Scott, Y. K., 1991. *The Habit of Surviving*. New York: Ballantine Books.

Tinsley, B. R. and Parke, R., 1984. "Grandparents as Support and Socialization Agents." In M. Lewis, ed., *Beyond the Dyad*. New York: Plenum.

White, D. G., 1985. *Ain't I a Woman? Female Slaves in the Plantation South*. New York: Norton.

Chapter 13

Sibling Relationships Among Older Adults

Martha Sebastian Moyer

Not enough attention is paid by professionals or the lay public to sibling relationships among the elderly (Suggs, 1989). In fact, these relationships assume, or reassume, crucial importance in the lives of older adults (Bedford, 1989a). After young adult siblings leave home to establish their own life, the relationship between them often goes underground until they are older (Banks and Kahn, 1982).

No two sibling relationships are alike. Their sensitive nature (Bedford, 1989b) makes sibling relationships hard to study and write about. Four out of five older adults have at least one remaining sibling and have frequent interaction with their brothers and sisters (Shanus, 1979). Sibling relationships are unique: Siblings share the same biological and cultural heritage, the longest relationships in terms of years, and many similar memories (Cicirelli, 1982). For many older adults, siblings are the only surviving support system.

This chapter will explore older adult sibling relationships in the following contexts or areas: caregivers for parents; caregivers for each other; reconciling past differences; friendship or estrangement; and death, changes in family structure and roles. Suggestions for enhancing and using sibling relationships as an important part of the support system for older adults will be discussed at the conclusion of the chapter. Not intended as a research report or an exhaustive review of professional literature, this chapter is based on professional observations made in more than 20 years as a multigenerational therapist, counseling older adults and their families and training professionals who work with older adults around the country.

CAREGIVERS FOR PARENTS

Unfortunately one of the first reasons older adult siblings again focus on their sibling relationships lies in the need to organize caregiving arrangements for their ailing parents. Wiping the sleep out of their eyes, the siblings have to refocus their attention on their family of origin (Banks and Kahn, 1982). Role and power reversals abound. The parents who loved and nurtured, or abused and manipulated, them now need help.

When there is more than one adult child in the family, caring for parent(s) has an impact on all siblings (Matthews and Rosner, 1988). Siblings who may have had little to do with each other find themselves in more frequent contact as they work to coordinate the direct care or care arrangements for their parent(s). Unless a family is very close, older adult children usually strive to hold to the "principle of the least involvement," which saves the independence of both generations for as long as possible (Matthews and Rosner, 1988).

What is the impact of caring for parents on older adult siblings? Who tends to do the caring? Researchers find that having one daughter is a key to receiving help (Spitze and Logan, 1990). Few families were without their tensions, and most of the stress came from premorbid problems between the siblings. Most siblings worked to keep their problems with each other from upsetting the parental care arrangements (Matthews and Rosner, 1988).

Andrea's Family

Caring for their parents can renew and enhance the relationships among the older adult siblings. Before their 90-year-old father died of a stroke, Andrea's family of six older adult siblings had focused their attention on their immediate families for over 30 years. Still in shock over the death of their father, the older adult children found themselves faced with the task of helping their 80-year-old mother, who was seriously ill with cancer.

The older adult children were able to form their own "parental care plan." Honoring the mother's wish to stay in her home for as long as possible, the siblings who lived in the area took on the day-to-day hands-on care. Three out-of-town daughters, two of whom were retired, rearranged their lives so that they could visit several times a year for three weeks at a time to relieve the hometown sibling caregivers.

Because of the large number of siblings, Andrea's family was able to provide care for their mother without overwhelming their personal lives (Spitze and Logan, 1990). They supported each other as they dealt individually with their grief and fear of their own impending mortality.

They got to know each other as adults and were able to defuse petty grievances from childhood. This cooperation was their last tribute to their beloved dying mother.

Caring for ailing parent(s) does not always enhance relationships among older adult siblings. The stress of the caregiving and the parent's illness will break through the veneer of politeness, covering the anger that underlies many sibling relationships. Unresolved sibling issues can poison sibling relationships for generations (Bedford, 1989b).

Monica

Monica, age 74, a successful business woman and divorced mother of four, was referred for evaluation because of her depression. One of three siblings born to a wealthy Montana rancher and his wife, Monica had just lost her mother, who had died of a stroke at the age of 96. (Her father had died some years earlier.) Both of Monica's parents had been children of alcoholics and tried to compensate for this humiliation by putting together, for themselves and their children, a lifestyle that was successful and respectable.

Monica was the family scapegoat who, although she herself did not drink, had married and divorced three different alcoholics. She was written in and out of the parents' will as they passed judgment on her lifestyle. Her older brother and sister were the "good and responsible " siblings in their parents' eyes (and will).

During her mother's final illness, Monica tried to go home and help with the caregiving. Her mother and siblings would not permit her to help with the mother's care. Neither the parent nor the "good siblings" could handle Monica's request to be allowed "emotionally" back into the family. To do so would have destabilized the family's homeostasis, which had held the family 's emotional process together all these years (Banks and Kahn, 1982).

When the mother died, Monica received only a few personal effects of her parents. As a result, she would not speak to her siblings or allow any of her adult children to have anything to do with her siblings' families. Monica and her siblings were unable to use a final caregiving opportunity to surmount decades of family relationship problems.

CAREGIVERS FOR EACH OTHER

Various studies have shown that siblings can function as an insurance policy for older adults (Avioli, 1989; Slade, 1991). The demographics of the American family are changing caregiving patterns. The growth in the number of single elders and the geographic mobility of adult children (especially those who are childless) increase the need for siblings to be part of each other's social support systems (Bedford, 1989a).

Research results are mixed in the area of siblings as caregivers. Having peer or same generational status was found to give siblings more empathy for and identification with their ailing brothers and sisters (Avioli, 1989). Although some elderly siblings provide direct assistance for each other, they are much more likely to socialize with each other (O'Bryant, 1988; Scott, 1983). Bedford (1989a) was surprised to discover in her research that for some older adult siblings, giving or receiving help was distressful.

Bill and Jim

Bill, age 90, who had outlived his wife and son, and his brother Jim, age 95, who was single and suffering from multiple sclerosis, lived together in a small apartment. Despite his own infirmities, Bill did all of the physical care for Jim, whose more adequate retirement income paid the bulk of their expenses. Resisting the efforts of the helping professionals from the local senior services program to place Jim in a skilled nursing facility, they reported that they would rather "die than be separated from each other." Eventually they went into a skilled nursing facility together.

Bill and Jim's relationship met Avioli's test of a good elderly sibling caregiving relationship: "balanced reciprocity—optional rather then obligatory exchange of supports" (1989). Bill provided the physical care and Jim provided the major financial support. Bill and Jim's closeness would be surprising to one researcher who found that brothers were the least likely to help each other in times of need—that two sisters were the most supportive and helpful to each other (O'Bryant, 1988). Bill and Jim's lack of living adult children may have added to their need to care for each other.

Some siblings can be resentful, reluctant caregivers. Often forced to step in when their older adult siblings' own spouses or children are deceased or unwilling to help, they often feel stuck. Sisters who were becoming more "independent" resented the need to care for a sibling— especially a brother (Bedford, 1989a). This is especially true if the two older adult siblings were not close as children or younger adults. Susan was a good example of this problem.

Susan and Martha

Susan grew up in the shadow of her more talented sister, Martha, who was a famous professor at Columbia University. Martha often let Susan know what a "drab life" she (Susan) lived. Susan married, had two children, and looked forward to a quiet retirement with her husband, Henry. When she was 77, Martha became ill with a brain tumor and returned to the hometown so that Susan, her only sibling, could take care of her. She treated Susan like a servant. Henry and Susan's adult children were enraged and demanded that Susan place Martha in a skilled nursing facility.

Torn between these two loyalties, Susan became quite depressed. With counseling, she was empowered to tell Martha that she would visit her but could not physically or emotionally handle Martha's direct care. Surprisingly, Martha was able to hear her, and with increased respect for her sister, agreed to go into a skilled nursing facility. Now a visiting caregiver by choice, Susan willingly spent much time with her sister. Both sisters became emotionally closer before Martha died six months later.

RECONCILING PAST DIFFERENCES

The older adult years can provide siblings who have been estranged from each other with a rich opportunity—and, of course, their last chance—to move toward reconciliation. Even older adult siblings who have had superficially close relationships often find that the later years can be a time of increased closeness and sharing (Bedford, 1989a). But not always. One researcher, Stephen Banks, expressed it this way: "As siblings grow older, good relationships become better and rotten relationships get worse" (quoted in Kutner, 1990).

Sometimes, especially in dysfunctional families, both parents need to die before older adult siblings can begin to reconcile with each other. These parents had kept their children, since infancy, in emotional bondage by withholding approval, love, and other types of validation. As a result, the children were competitive with and alienated from each other into their older adult years. Sometimes such a situation can carry over into rivalries between the nuclear families of each sibling.

Jim and Bill, for example, had been very estranged from each other before their parents died. Their mother, their last remaining parent, had always held Bill "up to Jim" as the "ideal son." Jim had spent much of his adult life trying to compete with Bill in his mother's eyes. After her death, the brothers, then in their 70s, spent some time with each other. Jim discovered that Bill envied his (Jim's) freedom from having to carry the burden of the mother's high expectations for him. Both brothers vowed to make up for the lost time and became very close, as we saw in the earlier case example.

Family secrets that have been maintained for decades can block closeness with and communication between older adult siblings. When these secrets are brought into the open, especially secrets about incest, alcoholism, and parental extramarital affairs, older adult siblings will often be freed from the burden of secrecy. Older adult siblings can be very helpful to each other as they each struggle to heal and process their experience.

Julio, Maria, and Paulina

All in their 60s, Julio, Maria and Paulina experienced rather superficial relationships with each other until the death of their father, their remaining parent. Soon after that, Maria began to experience memories, for the first time, of being sexually assaulted during her teenage years by the father. Unable to handle the memories by herself, she reluctantly sought professional help. Advised by her therapist to ask her siblings for confirmations of these memories, she was startled to learn that Paulina had suffered a similar fate during her teenage years. Julio had known what was happening to his sisters but had been threatened with death by the father if he said or did anything about it. Each sibling had handled his or her part of this heavy secret by avoiding emotional closeness with each other.

The opening up of this family secret allowed the siblings to support and finally to get to know each other as they worked on their individual and family healing. Older adult siblings are pressured by the acknowledgment of their own mortality to seek reconciliation with each other. Others are encouraged or pleaded with by dying parents to make peace with a sibling. Many older adult siblings help each other come to terms with their life by helping each other process and come to terms with their early life experiences in their family of origin. Others are not so fortunate. They never find the maturity to resolve their problems with their siblings (Bedford, 1989b).

FRIENDSHIP OR ESTRANGEMENT

Connidis (1989) complained that the subject of siblings as close friends is not examined as much as that of sibling rivalry. Older adult siblings often form one of the strongest social support systems for the older adult during the good times as well as the bad. It is at this time that many older adult siblings rediscover each other as travel companions, as a source of emotional support, and as fellow travelers back into the land of family memories and nostalgia. Seventy-four percent of older adults consider at least one of their siblings to be a close friend (Avioli, 1989).

Mary and Her Sisters

Mary, a 75-year-old new widow, was very emotionally close to her adult children and grandchildren. Despite this, she decided to return to her Ohio hometown to be closer to her two sisters, also widows. After much consultation among the three family units, the three sisters sold their own homes and bought a single residence that had enough room for all of them and their favorite possessions. Later, when they began to need personal care, they pooled their financial resources and hired in-home help, which enabled them to live independently for 10 more years. Better yet, their adult children, "the cousins," were able to take turns being available for additional emotional and physical help on an as-needed basis as the years went on.

Early life relationship problems between older adult siblings and their brothers- or sisters-in-law can effectively keep older adult siblings from maintaining or regaining closeness in their later years.

Sean, Nina, and Marlene

Sean, Nina, and Marlene were reasonably close to each other during their childhood years. As young adults, they became very close since they lived in the same metropolitan area and saw one another often.

When Sean married Jan, both sisters were upset by Jan's narcissistic behavior and by her later emotional abuse of her children. Jan, in turn, was jealous of Sean's former close relationship with his sisters. This early conflict permeated the siblings' relationship for the rest of their lives. Sean saw little of his sisters and joined his family only for the ritualized visits common to many older adult siblings (Avioli, 1989).

In discussing siblings as friends, we should not neglect the reverse of that phenomenon, namely, friends as siblings. Only children, siblings like Sean who cannot surmount their relationship problems, and others who have had to cut themselves off from severely dysfunctional families, must form their own support system with friends.

Many siblings often live very far from each other during much of their adult lives. They, too, must thus look to friends as family. Others who develop educational, religious, economic, and political differences with their older adult siblings find that their friends are the ones they turn to in their older adult years for companionship and help.

DEATH, CHANGES IN FAMILY STRUCTURE AND ROLES

The first death among older adult siblings has a profound effect on each sibling. It is a break in the mental and emotional armor that protects them from their own sense of mortality. Much more has been made of the impact of the death of parents on older adults. The first and subsequent death of siblings removes or reduces any chance for siblings who are emotionally distanced from each other to become close. Each death also removes one more member of our childhood memory data bank—someone who knew us when we were young and energetic. These memories can serve as a buffer for many older adults as they grapple with some of the harder aspects of aging.

As older adult siblings begin to die, the sibling constellation changes profoundly. Younger members or the youngest in a large family can become the oldest—or can become an only child upon the death of the last older sibling.

Manuel

Manuel, age 78, was the third youngest in a family that originally had 12 children. When he heard of the death of his last remaining older sibling, a brother, he was silent and then said to his wife, "Anita, this means that I am now the oldest." It was a very sad and sobering experience for him and his immediate family.

The loss of parents or a sibling can cause families to regroup and put new emphasis on the older adult siblings' relationships with each other. If the parent or deceased sibling was the "emotional gatekeeper or social organizer for the family," remaining siblings are faced with the task of rewiring their relationship circuits. Some families are unable to do this and become or remain very emotionally distant from each other. This is also seen in the case where the "responsible" parents of older siblings die, leaving behind them older adult siblings who must take over these roles.

A sibling who is dying can often teach the remaining siblings about what to expect when their turn comes.

David

Dying of cancer, David, age 75, stayed close to his sister, age 77, and brother, age 80. He shared his inner feelings, reminisced with them about their childhood, and validated their importance in his life. After a struggle, he accepted his impending death and encouraged them not to be afraid when their time came to die.

CONCLUSION

Because of ageism or lack of information about multigenerational relationships, many helping professionals do not encourage their older adult clients to explore and better utilize sibling relationships. Lifelong unresolved sibling issues can stand in the way of older adult siblings being able to help each other and enjoy each other's company. This results in the sibling support system being underutilized by both the siblings and the helping professionals.

Ways in which the latter can work on the problem include the following:

1. When assessing the caregiving support system for an ailing parent or older adult sibling, practitioners should evaluate the complicated sibling dynamics before coming to any premature conclusions about what is going on.
2. Practitioners should be knowledgeable about and have worked on their feelings about their own sibling relationships to avoid having their unresolved countertransference issues prevent them from doing an accurate and sensitive intervention in this area for their older adult clients.

3. Practitioners should not assume that because their client is an older adult, his or her feelings about sibling relationship problems are not important and there is nothing that can be done. Although some older adult sibling relationships cannot be improved, older adult clients should be given the benefits of the same expertise, respect, and interest that would be given a younger client.

* * *

Martha Sebastian Moyer, L.C.S.W., B.C.D., is a professional trainer in gerontology; an instructor, graduate School of Social Work, California State University, Long Beach; patient services director, Greater Los Angeles Chapter, ALS Association; and maintains a private clinical practice in Los Angeles.

REFERENCES

Avioli, R., 1989. "The Social Support Functions of Siblings in Later Life." *American Behavioral Scientist* 33 (1): 45–57.

Banks, S. and Kahn, M., 1982. *The Sibling Bond*. New York: Basic Books.

Bedford, V., 1989a. "Understanding the Value of Siblings in Old Age." *American Behavioral Scientist* 33(1): 33–44.

Bedford, V., 1989b. "Ambivalence in Adult Sibling Relationships." *Journal of Family Issues* 10(2):211–24.

Cicirelli, V., 1982. "Sibling Influence Throughout the Life Span." In Michael E. Lamb and Brian Sutton-Smith, eds., *Sibling Relationships: Their Nature and Significance Across the Life Span*. Hillsdale, N.J.: Lawrence Associates, pp. 267–84.

Connidis, I., 1989. "Siblings as Friends in Later Life." *American Behavioral Scientist* 33 (1):81–83.

Kutner, L., 1990. "Parent and Child: The Death of a Parent Can Profoundly Alter the Relations of Adult Siblings." *New York Times*, 6 Dec., p. C8.

Matthews, S. and Rosner, T., 1988. "Shared Filial Responsibility: The Family as the Primary Caregiver." *Journal of Marriage and Family* 50: 185–95.

O'Bryant, S., 1988. "Sibling Support and Older Widows' Well-Being." *Journal of Marriage and the Family* 50:173–83.

Scott, J., 1983. "Siblings and Other Kin." In Timothy H. Brubaker, ed., *Family Relationships in Later Life*. Beverly Hills, Calif.: Sage, pp.47–62.

Shanus, E., 1979. "The Family as a Social Support System in Old Age." *Gerontologist* 19: 169–74.

Slade, M., 1991. "Siblings: Growing Up and Closer." *New York Times*, 25 July, pp. C1, C10.

Spitze, G. and Logan, J., 1990. "Sons, Daughters, and Intergenerational Social Support." *Journal of Marriage and the Family* 52: 420–30.

Suggs, P., 1989. "Predictors of Association Among Older Siblings." *American Behavioral Scientist* 33(1): 70–80.

Chapter 14

'Creating' Families: Older People Alone

Bonnie Genevay

Anna had outlived her only son by 20 years. She had lost track of her grandson, who had been in prison a thousand miles away, and her last sister had died some years before. She was without blood kin. But Anna had a powerful need to belong to someone, and so she "created" her own family. She called her case manager Son, whether he liked it or not. "Now, Son," she would say, "you get out of this business of taking care of poor people—except for me, of course. You find you a line of work where you can make some money! Then we'll take us a trip over to Washtucna, and see how many people we know buried in the cemetery there." Anna instructed the latchkey child in the apartment next to hers as if his very life depended on it, and it may have at times. And she adopted a proprietary air with the manager of her garden apartment complex, consulting with her about hair color; advising her how to get rid of the "dope fiends" and just plain mean people; and presenting her with cookies, sometimes with a gray hair baked in because of impaired vision.

Older people alone are living longer, too, and it is critical for policy makers, practitioners, and administrators to reframe the meaning of family with them in mind. Trainers in gerontology are increasingly being asked, "How do you define 'family'?" And it is an excellent question, for it affects *what* services we provide, *how* we provide them, and *how much power* we give older people to come up with people and strategies to meet their own needs (Freeman, 1981). For older people alone, "family" may be those significant people they have access to and choose to include in their circle of intimate others, regardless of blood or marriage ties. In "Where Have All the Families Gone?" David Bloom (1992) tells us that *the* American family does not exist; that we are creating *many* American families, of diverse styles and shapes. Despite these historic changes in American family life, the Gallup Poll reported in 1991 that 93 percent of respondents said that family life was "very important" to them.

What is curious to me is that in the media, families are seldom seen in the context of older family members, except in the aftermath of elder abuse, "granny dumping," or "grandpa abandonment"—as happened when 82-year-old John Kingery was abandoned at a dog-racing track in Idaho (Egan, 1992). In a most thorough article on "The New American Family" (Suro, 1991), the family is basically described in terms of young families: single parents, childless couples, broken families, traditional working and nonworking families. The author goes as far into the life developmental cycle as post-empty-nest parents helping their adult children by taking them back in, but does not include caregiving for elderly parents. Yet we know from Older Women's League data, and from the rapid growth of employee assistance eldercare programs and caregiver support groups, that older adult children may now spend more of their lives taking care of elderly than they did raising children. We now need to research all the ingenious, creative, and manipulative ways older people alone get their caregiving needs met. Creating "genuine fake families," in Virginia Satir's words, is a great way to maintain a little power over life and to be selective in choosing those you want around you as you become more frail and die.

My experience with this population—older people alone—is that professional helpers are either traumatized because there are *no* family members to provide support, or traumatized because there *are* family members who do not provide enough support, the "right kind" of support, or who provide no support at all. There are, however, a vast array of nonblood "kin" who act as surrogate family for many elderly people. They include friends (longstanding and new), neighbors, former unmarried partners and ex-in-laws, volunteers, church members, and professional health and social service providers.

It is crucial that all these helpers (nurses, social workers, counselors, court workers, home health aides, and outreach workers, among many others) *do not* take on a surrogate family role when they are highly stressed on the job and would have to sacrifice self-care and family life to do so. The care provider needs to look at the unfilled needs of the older client who has cast her or him in the role of "good son" or "good daughter" and to understand the transference or countertransference that contributes to "adopting" an older person as a quasi-family member (Genevay and Katz, 1990). If assumed, it is a contract not unlike marriage *used* to be: "till death do us part." Choosing to adopt an older person alone, and taking on personal as well as professional commitments, has more to do with life energy, freedom from guilt, and choice than it does with patronization of "those poor old people who are all alone." We may be responding to our own fears of being alone at the end of life rather than realistically assessing what we can actually take on. Older people choose us for their own reasons, and we can say "yes" or "no"—depending on whether we can fulfill our commitment. It is the job of old people alone to create their own new families; it is the job of care providers to know when they can and when they cannot take on such a role.

HOW DO OLDER PEOPLE ALONE CREATE A SURROGATE FAMILY?

Evelyn's siblings had preceded her in death by some 20 years. She had never been married or had children, and the family members she had communed with daily were grandparents, of whom she had been very fond, her parents, and a sister she had been close to. Evelyn was not demented in any way, but in her mind she "talked to" family members long gone and was deeply influenced in her current values and behavior by what they might think of her now. Evelyn had always been a private person, and when her last close friend died, she didn't nourish new friendships. As she became more frail and had to depend on someone, she connected with a volunteer of a cancer support program. Even though she was medicated for pain, she did not lose hold of her fine mind and knew that this volunteer was *not* her sister, but would say, "You are as much my sister as anyone could be!" Evelyn chose not to die alone, and asked her new sister to be with her. This was a very significant relationship for both of them, even though it lasted only three years.

Harry was a genial, loving man in his late 80s. He did odd jobs and, with several other elders, was asked to be part of a panel discussion on housing needs. He found himself able to talk about his parents, his hardships during the Depression, the loss of his beloved wife, and how sad he was at the distance between himself and his children who lived "as far as you could get" across the country from him. Participation on this panel turned out to be an opportunity for life review, and he "fell in love" with two of the staff of the agency sponsoring the panel. From then on he volunteered at the agency so that he could see them regularly. He proffered social invitations to these two staff members, and one of them continued a close relationship with him until he died. Harry tried to proposition the other staff member, an older woman, but she gently and gracefully said no, which he accepted with good humor. He then offered his affection to a neighbor who was willing and able to reciprocate.

Lucille had grown up in a family beset by violence, illness, victimization, and loss. Yet she had carefully honed her own personal philosophy of "I'll do the best I can, one day at a time." When Lucille retired from her government job, she decided to be good to herself, for she had worked very hard freeing herself of faithless husbands, raising other family members' children, and caring for and burying loved ones through the years. She bought the largest screen TV she could afford and surrounded herself with "family" who couldn't reach through the screen and hit her, blame their pain on her, or demand that she fix their problems. Lucille was an armchair psychologist to her favorite family members in the afternoon soaps, and she often said "I told you so" to all the characters who didn't listen to her advice. She was enamored of Sidney Poitier and Harry Belafonte in their early movies, and made Bill Cosby's family her very own. (They had such benign problems compared to her family's.) Lucille was always polite to human-service workers, who offered what they thought she needed, and gracious to neighbors, but categorically said no to senior services. Some people were irritated when she did not answer the phone or when she said, "I can't talk right now." They sensed that Lucille's TV programs were more important to her than anything they might say. One professional labeled her delusional and depressed, but there was no evidence that she was not functioning well, for her house was clean and her nutrition good. Lucille had simply created family members who stayed at a safe distance of four feet; she enjoyed them very much, and she did not invest in flesh and blood relationships again.

Sara was in her 90s, an elegant and cultured lady with bluing in her wavy white hair. She had "divorced" her three sons and their families 30 years ago, when they failed to behave toward her as she thought they should. She did not like her daughters-in-law and felt that her sons had been given far more than they had ever given in return. When Sara first came to a therapy group for older people, she related only to the therapist and refused to form relationships with other group members. She often stayed after group and told the therapist in no uncertain terms that she was the "good daughter" Sara had never had. Eventually Sara became disenchanted and left the group because she did not get the personal affection and attention she so badly needed and wanted. Over a period of years, she sought surrogate family relationships with a number of professionals of various kinds, and always felt rejected because they did not give her as much as she needed. She died alone in the emergency ward of a hospital.

WHAT LEADS OLDER PEOPLE ALONE TO CREATE NEW FAMILIES?

Life circumstances and the desire to resolve and rectify them, as well as the absence of family patterns and relationships that were satisfying, contribute to the search by older people for new intimacy, trust, safety, and inclusion. Achieving integrity rather than despair as an end task of life may well depend on filling some of the holes that blood kin family relationships left empty. Some circumstances that motivate older people to try to create new families, as we saw with Evelyn, Harry, Lucille, and Sara, are (1) being alone, without spouse, children, or other living relatives; (2) being geographically isolated, with children, grandchildren, or other relatives hundreds or thousands of miles away who cannot fulfill the emotional, physical, or psychological needs and expectations of older people alone; (3) being part of a dysfunctional family or having a personal life of adversity and needing to recover from painful relationships; and (4) being unable to let go of blaming and punishing behavior toward family who have not lived up to expectations. There are combinations of these circumstances and many others that could be cited. Whatever the situation, older people alone have legitimate grounds for trying to reinvent their lives with new characters and for attempting to fill the emptiness if they can.

Professional helpers of all kinds need to understand what is behind older people's desire for more (or fewer) services, more (or less) time and attention, and more (or less) personal care than seems warranted by the facts, diagnosis, or assessment. Beyond understanding, we need to shape clearly our own limits and boundaries so that we can honor the needs of older people alone and not promise more than we can reasonably give. The ethics involved in becoming a personal friend or surrogate family member are far more complex than professional guidelines in a staff policy manual, and they have much more to do at times with our own needs and values than with our job descriptions. There is no alternative for good supervision and consultation when it comes to adopting an older client or colluding with that person's wish that we become family.

WHAT THEMES RECUR FOR THE
OLDER PERSON ALONE?

Feelings about mortality and finishing of life, personal regrets, need for forgiveness and to say "I'm sorry," and expressions of love for dead family members as well as living are frequently mentioned in life review. Both the spontaneous life review that emerges when staff take time to listen to the older person alone, and the intentional life review that occurs during music therapy, art therapy, journal-writing, and tape-recorded memories, are valuable tools for defining and resolving family relationship issues. Many times the intimacy that develops between a care provider and a patient is the direct result of having shared grief over past difficulties. The relief and trust that follow may enable the older person to invest in a "new" family attachment to the care provider. This does not mean that helpers should avoid evoking and listening to life review; it is to say that great care and responsibility are involved in working with past family issues.

The tasks of all the developmental stages of life seem to reach a crescendo for many older people alone, and each task seems to arise again for one final placement in the mosaic of a life. Several years ago I shared Erikson's developmental stages and tasks with 80 retired businessmen. They were polite, receptive, and noncommittal as I wrote the following on the flipchart: trust, autonomy, intimacy, identity, generativity, integrity. Then I asked them what tasks they thought they were still working on, postretirement. They looked at me as if I might not be too bright. "It's elemental," one said. "*All* of the above, of course!" another said. There seemed to be consensus, and I learned a great deal from their comments: "I'm trying to trust my kids all over again; it wasn't easy when they were 15 and it's harder now when they're 50." "Do you know how difficult it is to be independent and autonomous when you use a cane and wear Depends?" "I don't know if I'll ever be close to anyone again; I just lost my wife of 48 years." "Work was everything to me; now that my career's gone, I don't know who I am." "I'm trying to find something about life that excites me as much as work did." "I still need to be a good friend or a good person to *someone*."

This last statement struck me hard. Older people alone have the right to be part of a family. They have choices: they can repair relationships with their own blood kin if they have any; they can grieve for and let go of relationships that cannot be changed; *or* they can move on to new relationships with surrogate family members who are related by liking, affinity, and mutual exchange. Helping professionals need to (1) broaden the definition of family to include significant others as defined by the older client; (2) reflect on our own definition of "family" and how it affects the work we do; (3) consider carefully whether we can or cannot accept a particular older person's invitation to become immediate family; and (4) respect and admire the creativity—even if we do not agree with the ways—that older people alone use to reconstitute their families.

Remember that Webster defines a surrogate as "a person 'appointed' to act in place of another." An older patient or client may *appoint* you a family substitute, but you have a clear responsibility to choose whether or not you can fulfill that surrogate role. If you cannot, the process provides a wonderful opportunity to help the older person alone work through end-of-life issues.

*   *   *

Bonnie Genevay, M.S.W., is a Seattle-based trainer and consultant in gerontology and bereavement, and coauthor with Renée Katz, Ph.D., of Countertranference and Older Clients.

REFERENCES

Bloom, D., 1992. "Where Have All the Families Gone?" *The Source* 17(1), Supplement.

Egan, T., 1992. "When Children Can't Afford Parents." *New York Times,* 29 Mar., E 7.

Freeman, D., 1981. *Techniques of Family Therapy.* New York: Jason Aronson.

Genevay, B. and Katz, R., 1990. *Countertransference and Older Clients.* Newbury Park, Calif.: Sage.

Suro, T., 1991. "The New American Family: Reality Is Wearing the Pants." *New York Times,* 29 Dec., E 2.

Chapter 15

Family Caregiving Programs: A Look at the Premises on Which They Are Based

Greta Berry Winbush

Family caregiving has received much attention within the last decade. Family caregiving encompasses an array of issues involving the care of dependent family members, cutting across diverse perspectives. The issues on which researchers, practitioners, and policy makers have focused have ranged from concerns about the primary caregiver (e.g., Stone, Cafferata and Sangl, 1987) to questions about the effectiveness of social service programs in meeting the growing demands of family caregiving (Caserta et al., 1987; Burdz, Eaton and Bond, 1988; Green and Monahan, 1989; Lawton, Brody and Saperstein, 1989; Montgomery and Borgatta, 1989; Berry, Zarit and Rabatin, 1991), to concerns about cost-containment or reduced government involvement when the economy is in trouble.

It is this diversity that provokes one to question the premises for family caregiving programs. For example, are family caregiving programs based on a view that family caregiving is a longtime norm of family functioning, or a new phenomenon? Do they respond to a view that family caregiving is functioning well with current levels of support, or are they based on perceptions of a caregiving crisis?

In fact, families have long been supportive of their members, providing care to those who were dependent (Shanas, 1979; Cantor, 1985).

Family caregiving is not a new phenomenon but is considered a norm of the family and is based on familial and societal obligations. This norm of family caregiving has been enforced in some states through family responsibility laws (Callahan et al., 1980).

Longtime norm or not, family caregiving is currently in a state of crisis, according to many. Another question then arises: Does this crisis attitude stem from a fear that families are abandoning their responsibilities or is it a response to a cry for help from families in need of assistance with their caregiving responsibilities?

In line with these orientations, it would seem that family caregiving programs do fall into two categories: (1) those aimed at providing supportive services to families, and (2) those with the goal of providing incentives to encourage family caregiving. This division reflects a number of new and not-so-new controversies: family versus public responsibility, institutional versus community supports, men's versus women's issues, and young versus old, to name a few. Controversies aside, it would seem that success or failure of family caregiving programs is inextricably related to the premise on which these programs are based.

When we consider the effectiveness of programs based on the "normative family functioning" orientation, we should refer to the theoretical frameworks (if any) for such programs. The question then becomes whether or not family caregiving programs are based on any family model or perspective of family functioning—normative or not. For example, Hill (1964) speaks of families having a life cycle similar to that of individuals. During this life cycle, the family undergoes development or change that is characterized by stages of behavior or life events. Caregiving could be considered a stage or life event within the family life cycle. However, while caregiving is only an event in the family's life cycle, our supportive and incentive strategies have extracted it from the total family picture and have treated it as a separate and individual—and often "societal"—event. More specifically, programs primarily have been directed toward the individual (i.e., caregiver or care receiver) rather than toward the family. By continuing to look at caregiving as an individual event, overlooking the total family context, we run into difficulties incorporating into program development aspects of family functioning like support networks.

Incorporated within the notion of a family life cycle is the idea that various events, including caregiving, could occur numerous times and at different points throughout the life cycle of the family. Programming should take into consideration the fact that at various points in the family life cycle, care needs are different, and consequently the required incentives and supports are equally diverse.

While the family life cycle is of great importance in program development, so is the conceptual thinking surrounding family composition. Social scientists often speak of two family types: family of origin and family of procreation. When considering the family of origin, we see that the potential for care provision and care demand is present through the various familial relations (i.e., parents, siblings, extended family, and fictive kin). For the family of procreation, similar caregiving situations are possible through family relationships such as spouse, children, and grandchildren.

In short, the opportunities and situations for family caregiving are many and diverse. However, despite their number and diversity, current thinking has been directed primarily toward later-adult caregiving situations. Most family caregiving programming has been reflective of this current train of thought.

When we examine "crisis-oriented" family caregiving programs, we should determine their effectiveness in light of perceptions about abandonment of family caregiving or need of caregiving assistance. In fact, families are not abandoning their caregiving responsibilities (Shanas, 1979; Brody, 1985), but they do need assistance in providing care. Perhaps this explains the lack of success seen in some of the "incentives for caregiving" program initiatives (e.g., tax stipends and paid caregivers); families have incentive, what they need is help.

Families today are faced with numerous new challenges not evident in the past, which raise questions about the families' ability to overcome—and to overcome without assistance. For example, family caregiving today is taking place in a societal setting characterized by changes in family composition, technological and social advances, life-threatening health problems, and a devalued attitude toward the family. These factors, separate or combined, have generated caregiving situations that were not so prevalent a few decades ago: children providing care for babies (teenage motherhood), men providing care for men (HIV-positive males), women providing care for adult children and grandchildren who are substance abusers or victims of substance abuse (crack cocaine and fetal alcohol syndrome babies), and care provision to a growing population of frail elderly.

Manifestations of the devalued attitude toward the family, for example, include high rates of divorce, unemployment, and poverty;

lack of or inadequate healthcare; substandard or no housing; hunger or malnutrition. Each of these factors has a serious impact on family functioning and adequate family-care provision. It is clear that current programming has been primarily directed toward the perceived traditional family (i.e., nuclear, middle class, white).

Given the many circumstances facing them today, it is evident that families need assistance in handling their caregiving responsibilities. However, the programs generated to meet these needs have stemmed primarily from the perceptions of social scientists, practitioners, and policy makers. Families are seldom asked what their specific needs are. Often, families play only a small role in decisions about timing, availability, and characteristics of support. It is no wonder that findings on the use and effectiveness of caregiving services are not always conclusive and positive.

CONCLUSION

In conclusion, family caregiving certainly warrants concern, but the approach to addressing this concern should be based on theoretical and empirical knowledge about the family and about the reality of family caregiving situations and needs. We need to be sure that the interpretations truly reflect the voices of these families. Most important is sensitivity to the diversity across and within family types. We should be sensitive to emerging family types, new challenges facing the family as a whole, and the fact that care needs or provision are not predicated on age alone.

In addition, we cannot, without detriment, continue to isolate events such as caregiving in the family life cycle and continue to ignore the total family context. It would be even more hazardous to do so given the fact that the timing of family life cycles and their nature are always changing as a result of technological and social developments, both good and bad.

Last, we need to be sensitive to the political and social problems that affect family functioning and its necessary supports. Such problems include manifestations of a devalued attitude toward the family; women's issues, which are often synonymous with family issues; the conflicts between age and need and between family and government. Sadly, continued ignorance of these social problems will only result in more family caregiving programs with fewer desired outcomes.

*   *   *

Greta Berry Winbush, Ph.D., is assistant professor of human development and aging policy, College of Social Work, Ohio State University, Columbus.

REFERENCES

Berry, G., Zarit, S. and Rabatin, V., 1991. "Caregiver Activity on Respite and Non-Respite Days." *Gerontologist* 31(6): 830–35.

Brody, E., 1985. "Parent Care as a Normative Stress." *Gerontologist* 25(1): 19–29.

Burdz, M., Eaton, W. and Bond, J., 1988. "Effects of Respite Care on Dementia and Nondementia Patients and Their Caregivers." *Psychology and Aging* 3(1):38–42.

Callahan, J. et al., 1980. "Responsibility of Families for the Severely Disabled Elders." *Health Care Financing Review* 1(13):29–48.

Cantor, M., 1985. "Families: A Basic Source of Long-Term Care for the Elderly." *Aging* 349:1–5.

Caserta et al., 1987. "Caregivers to Dementia Patients: The Utilization of Community Services." *Gerontologist* 27(2): 209–14.

Green, V. and Monahan, D., 1989. "The Effect of a Support and Education Program on Stress and Burden Among Family Caregivers to Frail Elderly Persons." *Gerontologist* 29(4): 472–77.

Hill, R., 1964. "Methodological Issues in Family Development Research." *Family Process* 3(2):186–206.

Lawton, M., Brody, E. and Saperstein, A., 1989. "A Controlled Study of Respite Service for Caregivers of Alzheimer's Patients." *Gerontologist* 29(1): 9–16.

Montgomery, R. and Borgatta, E., 1989. "The Effects of Alternative Support Strategies on Family Caregiving." *Gerontologist* 29(3): 457–64.

Shanas, E., 1979. "The Family as a Social Support System in Old Age." *Gerontologist* 19(2)169–74.

Stone, R., Cafferata, G. and Sangl, J., 1987. "Caregivers of the Frail Elderly: A National Profile." *Gerontologist* 27(5): 616–26.

Chapter 16

Families and Caregiving in an Aging Society*

Marjorie H. Cantor

Just as dynamic changes are occurring in the size, composition, and health status of the aging population, the American family is also undergoing transformations that will affectthe ability of families to provide care for their elder members. In this chapter the term *family* is used in its broadest sense to include the many varieties of family structure in which related and nonrelated individuals live together and function as family to each other, both instrumentally and emotionally. Only such a broad definition accurately captures how the care of older people occurs in a "family sense."

Furthermore, in considering the capacity of families to provide care for disabled elders, we are concerned not only with individual units but also with kin networks spanning several generations. The following trends in family structure may affect the continued ability of families to provide caregiving for impaired members (Bengtson, 1986; Bengtson, Rosenthal and Burton, 1990; Day, 1985; Hagestad, 1986, 1988).

- Multigenerational families are becoming the norm. By the year 2020, the typical family will consist of at least four generations.

*This chapter is an adaptation of portions of the Donald P. Kent Award Lecture, "Family and Community: Changing Roles in an Aging Society," by Majorie H. Cantor, which also appeared in The Gerontologist (vol. 31[3]: 337–46). Adapted with permission.

- Families today are becoming increasingly "vertical," that is, having a greater number of relationships that cross generational lines and fewer siblings and other age-peers within a single generation (Bengtson and Dannefer, 1987; Hagestad, 1986).

- Kin networks are increasingly becoming top-heavy, with more older family members than younger. For the first time in history, the average married couple has more parents than children (Preston, 1984).

- Because of lengthening life expectancy and lower birthrates, shifts are occurring in the time spent in various family roles. For example, middle generation women in the future will probably spend, on average, more years with parents over 65 than with children under 18 (Watkins, Menken and Bongaarts, 1987).

- As the period of childbearing becomes increasingly more concentrated, and age differences between first and last child narrow, the lines of demarkation between generations become sharper. Only rarely do we now hear of aunts or uncles the same age or younger than their nieces and nephews, a not-uncommon phenomenon at the turn of the century (Pullam, 1982).

- Alterations in the timing of childbearing, the increasing incidence of divorce and reconstructed or step-families, and single-parent families are affecting and complicating family structures (Riley, 1983).

SPOUSES AS CAREGIVERS

In much of the gerontological literature on caregiving, and certainly in the popular press, one gets the impression that informal caregivers are synonymous with adult children, mainly daughters. This has proved to be a gross oversimplification of caregiving patterns. Actually, all research indicates that in most cases, the caregiver will be the spouse if one is available and capable; otherwise, children will assume the caregiving role. Our own research with caregivers in New York City suggests that spouses are a singularly important group who often carry a substantial portion of the support function, probably suffer more from strain, and about whom we know relatively little (Cantor, 1983).

The findings from two national samples of disabled elders and their caregivers illustrate the emerging role of spouse (Stephens and Christianson, 1986; Stone and Kemper, 1989). In both cases, spouses were major actors. Of the 4.2 million active caregivers in the 1984 National

Long Term Care Survey, 1.6 million were spouses, and in the National Long Term Care Channeling Demonstration, spouses made up almost one-quarter of the caregiver sample. Furthermore, the Long Term Care Survey found that spouses were far more likely to be the primary caregivers, with children acting predominantly as secondary caregivers.

And caregiving spouses are not only women; husbands caring for wives is a phenomenon of increasing importance—and one that has tended to be overlooked. Soldo and her associates (1990) note that in the 1982 National Long Term Care Survey, 85 percent of disabled married women who lived with their husbands were dependent upon them for personal care.

What about the future? Although incoming cohorts of elderly will probably include more "never married," as well as larger numbers of unrelated persons living as family, there is no evidence to suggest that the principle on which selection of primary caregiver is based will be altered in the future. Thus, where a spouse exists we can expect this wife or husband to serve as principal caregiver. With more men expected to live to older ages in the decades ahead, it is likely that the spouse as caregiver will be even more important in the future and that elderly couples will play a more significant role in family life (whether such couples are composed of original partners or result from remarriage in later life).

However, a word of caution about the caregiving capacities of such old-old couples is in order. As a concomitant of increased age and greater prevalence of morbidity, many of the older spouses may, themselves, be impaired and unable to provide extensive assistance with activities of daily living without help from either children or the formal sector. Thus, although there may be more couples, the pool of active spouse caregivers may not increase proportionately, and children may increasingly find themselves responsible for two frail or disabled parents who are attempting to care for each other.

ADULT CHILDREN AS CAREGIVERS

Today

We turn now to adult children, the principal caregivers of older women, no-longer-married women and men, and the secondary caregivers in situations where spouses are still alive. According to an analysis by Stone and Kemper (1989) of the 1984 National Long Term Care Survey, a minimum of 7 percent of all adults in the United States are either spouses or children of disabled elderly and therefore are potentially involved in caregiving decisions. The vast majority of these potential caregivers are adult children between the ages of 45 and 64. At present, the single age cohort most affected by caregiving responsibilities are the 45–54 year olds, with 17 percent of this age group having a disabled older parent.

Looking only at those actively involved in caregiving, we find that about 2.7 million adult children provide "hands-on care" of disabled elders. However, the 1984 Long Term Care Survey also discovered that adult children were more likely to be found as secondary rather than primary caregivers. This may come as a surprise, given the extensiveness of gerontological literature concerning the primacy of the role of adult children, but it reflects the previously mentioned fact that where spouses are available, they are generally the major source of care (Cantor, 1980; Shanas, 1979). But, even as secondary caregivers, adult children are vital sources of back-up and respite services to parents, as well as filling important social and emotional needs. In addition, research suggests that children frequently serve as family financial managers and intermediaries to formal services (Cantor, 1979, 1980; Cantor, Brook and Mellor, 1986; Chappell, 1985; Horowitz, 1985).

The importance of adult children is further illustrated by the National Long Term Channeling Demonstration. In that sample of only primary caregivers, about one-half were children or children-in-law, while one-quarter were spouses, with the remainder distributed among relatives, friends/neighbors, and paid help (Stephens and Christianson, 1986). Thus, although children are not always the major caregivers, they are usually part of the caregiving network, and it is children more than any other group who are the caregivers of elderly widowed women, the largest single component of the disabled elderly population.

Competing Responsibilities

Two competing responsibilities, childcare and employment, are usually cited with respect to family caregivers, particularly adult children. The 1984 Long Term Care Survey elucidates these potential sources of conflict, and the popular press has made much of the dual responsibilities faced by women of the "sandwich" generation. Actually, however, childcare and eldercare duties affect far fewer women than might be expected. The 1984 National Long Term Care Survey found that only about 7 percent of all women in the United States with children under age 15 were potentially faced with eldercare responsibilities in addition to care of children (Stone and Kemper, 1989). Furthermore, many less—436,000 women, or only 2 percent of U. S. mothers with young children—were actively involved in providing eldercare, and a much smaller group (only 164,000) served as primary caregivers. Other research also reports a similar picture regarding child and eldercare responsibilities (Boyd and Treas, 1989; Scharlach and Boyd, 1989; Stone, Cafferata and Sangl, 1987).

Although conflicts between care of children and adult parents can pose serious problems for the individuals involved, such conflicts are far less pervasive than might be thought. Almost two-thirds of the daughters in the Long Term Care sample were either middle-aged or elderly themselves, and they were more likely to be grandmothers than mothers of young children. What is more, this trend toward caregiving at an older age is expected to continue, further minimizing the likelihood of overlapping childcare and eldercare responsibilities. However, in some inner-city communities, particularly among African Americans and other minority groups, the number of grandparents with both eldercare and childcare responsibilities is on the increase.

The impact of employment on caregiving is more pervasive and potentially more serious. The 1984 Long Term Care Survey suggests that one-half of the spouses and children of disabled elders—over 7.4 million persons—are working full time. They represent about 9 percent of the full-time employed population of the United States. Forty-three percent of the daughters and wives of disabled people and 69 percent of the sons and husbands work full time (Stone and Kemper, 1989). Furthermore, among employed caregivers, 1.5 million (or 2 percent of the total full-time work force in the United States) are actively involved in providing assistance with activities of daily living, and close to 40 percent of the active caregivers carry the primary care responsibility. In line with many findings regarding the preeminent role of women in eldercare, women working full time are four times as likely to be primary caregivers as men (Stone and Kemper, 1989).

The National Long Term Care Demonstration Project reported an even higher proportion of employed persons among primary caregivers—34 percent were working. Of these, close to 70 percent were employed full-time (Stephens and Christianson, 1986). Whatever the exact numbers of employees with caregiving responsibilities, it is clear that a sizable segment of working adult children and some spouses must juggle work and eldercare as part of their everyday lives.

The potential for emotional, physical, and financial stress within such families is clearly present, to say nothing of the effect on the productivity of such doubly burdened workers.

The Future

In considering the role of adult children as caregivers in the future, several important trends need to be considered. First, and in some ways most crucial, is the later age at which most adult children will become involved in caregiving. With delay in the onset of morbidity, it is the young-old rather than 45–59 year olds who will increasingly be called upon to care for parents, as well as for older spouses. Most experts agree that while older people in the future will spend a longer time with chronic illnesses because of medical advances, earlier disease-detection, and changes in lifestyle, this longer time will often be accompanied by a slowing down in the process of the disease, its severity and disabling effects (Verbrugge, 1984). Thus, the period of severe disability is projected to move further up the life cycle, being most concentrated in what the English social historian Peter Laslett (1989) refers to as the Fourth Age, where the brunt of dependency needs will be felt. As a result, the majority of those over 85 will have need for assistance, while a smaller proportion of the middle-old, and even fewer of the young-old, will find themselves in a state of social-care dependency. Under such a scenario, although there will be larger numbers of older people, the "social-care curve" will probably shift upwards, and the age at which adult children will confront parent care will similarly rise.

Caregiving by adult children occurring later in the family life cycle could, of course, virtually eliminate competing childcare responsibilities and at least mitigate the conflict between employment and eldercare. However, there are several labor-force trends that could potentially minimize the availability of post-retirement-age adult children as caregivers. First is a projected rise in the official retirement age for Social Security. At present it is scheduled to start rising after the turn of the century, but there may be pressure to increase the age to 67 before that time. Currently, many workers leave the labor force before the existing official retirement age of 65 because of poor health, company retrenchment policies, or worker personal preference. However, it is expected that the population and the work force will grow more slowly in the next 15 years than at anytime since the 1930s, and the pool of younger workers, particularly those with requisite skills, will shrink (Johnston and Packer, 1987). This may provide a more conducive atmosphere for older workers to remain in the labor force longer as the need for skilled employees increases.

As a result, in line with improved health status and expectations of a high living standard, many younger elders may choose to remain in the work force longer. Retirement preferences are, however, influenced by social class and nature of employment. Therefore, the willingness to continue work longer will more likely affect business and professional occupations rather than factory and service industry jobs.

Furthermore, since women play so predominant a role in caregiving, their work patterns will be of great importance with respect to the availability of family caregivers. Over the next decade, it is expected that women will continue to enter the labor force in substantial numbers. By the year 2000, 48 percent of the work force will be women, and 61 percent of working-age women will be employed (Johnston and Packer, 1987).

Although women continue to be concentrated in traditionally female occupations, they are increasingly entering the business and professional worlds. In the past, a primary motivation for women working was the second salary to help pay for the education of children and a rising standard of living. Today increasing numbers of women are the sole support of families, and increasing numbers are more career-oriented, viewing their work as of tremendous personal importance. The work trajectory of women, many of whom enter the growth period of their careers later, may differ from that of men. And older women in the future may be even less willing or able to follow men out of the labor market than at present. Thus, working until their early or mid-70s may be far more common in the future, especially for women but also for men. This is a phenomenon that could restrict the availability of adult children as primary providers of hands-on care.

Other complicating trends bound to affect the availability of adult children as caregivers of parents include the decline in the average number of children per family and the increase in the number of nonmarried persons and childless couples.

Finally, future attitudes are a still-unknown factor that may radically influence the role of family members as providers of direct care. A key finding of the study of the elderly in the inner city of New York (Cantor, 1975), replicated in other studies as well, was the reluctance of older people to utilize formal care. For most respondents, such care was considered as a last resort when the informal system was nonexistent or unable to continue to provide the necessary assistance because of lack of requisite skills or competing responsibilities. In the 1970s, nursing homes were the primary alternative, and homecare was in its infancy and only for the rich. But many things have changed since then, not the least attitudes regarding appropriate sources of assistance.

The elderly coming into the aged cohorts are better educated, many have greater resources to purchase assistance, and there are intimations that they may feel differently regarding the use of services such as in-home care and adult daycare. Evidence of this shift was discernible in our recent study "Growing Old in Suburbia" (Cantor, Brook and Mellor, 1986) in which a representative sample of the "new" elderly were interviewed using the same instrument employed in the study of the inner city elderly of New York. The "new" elderly evidenced much greater willingness to consider turning to community formal agencies for assistance in the home, although they were as equally well-endowed with family and friend/neighbor networks as their inner city peers studied 15 years previously.

* * *

Marjorie H. Cantor, M.A., is University Professor and Brookdale Distinguished Scholar, Fordham University, New York.

REFERENCES

Bengtson, V., 1986. "Sociological Perspectives in Aging, Families and the Future." In M. Bergener, ed., *Perspective on Aging: The 1986 Sandoz Lectures in Gerontology.* New York: Academic Press.

Bengtson, V. and Dannefer, D., 1987. "Families, Work, and Aging: Implications of Disordered Cohort Flow for the 21st Century." In R. Ward and S. S. Tobin, eds., *Health in Aging: Sociological Issues and Policy Directions.* New York: Springer.

Bengtson, V., Rosenthal, C. and Burton, L., 1990. Families and Aging: Diversity and Heterogeneity. In R. H. Binstock and L. K. George, eds., *Handbook of Aging and the Social Sciences,* 3d ed. New York: Academic Press.

Boyd, S. L. and Treas, J., 1989. Family Care of the Frail Elderly: A New Look at 'Women in the Middle.' " *Women's Studies Quarterly* 17:66–74.

Cantor, M. H., 1975. "Life Space and the Social Support System of the Inner City Elderly of New York." *Gerontologist* 15:23–7.

Cantor, M. H., 1979. "Neighbors and Friends: An Overlooked Resource in the Informal Support System." *Research on Aging* 1:434–63.

Cantor, M. H., 1980. "The Informal Support System: Its Relevance in the Lives of the Elderly." In E. Borgatta and N. McClusky, eds., *Aging and Society*. Beverly Hills, Calif: Sage.

Cantor, M. H., 1983. "Strain Among Caregivers: A Study of Experience in the United States." *Gerontologist* 23:597–604.

Cantor, M. H., Brook, K. H. and Mellor, M. J., 1986. *Growing Old in Suburbia*. New York: Brookdale Research Institute, Third Age Center, Fordham University.

Chappell, N. L., 1985. "Social Support and the Receipt of Home Care Services." *Gerontologist* 25:47–54.

Day, A. T., 1985. "Who Cares? Demographic Trends Challenge Family Care for the Elderly." *Population Trends and Public Policy No. 9*. Washington, D.C.: Population Reference Bureau.

Hagestad, G. O., 1986. "The Aging Society as a Context for Family Life." *Daedalus* 115:119–39.

Hagestad, G. O., 1988. "Demographic Change and the Life Course: Some Emerging Trends in Family Realm." *Family Relations* 37:405–10.

Horowitz, A., 1985. "Family Caregiving to the Frail Elderly." In C. Eisdorfer, M. P. Lawton and G. Maddox, eds., *Annual Review of Gerontology and Geriatrics* 5: 194–246.

Johnston, W. and Packer, A., 1987. *Workforce 2000: Work and Workers for the Twenty-First Century*. Indianapolis, Ind.: Hudson Institute.

Laslett, P., 1989. *A Fresh Map of Life: The Emergence of the Third Age*. London: Weidenfeld and Nicolson.

Preston, S., 1984. "Children and the Elderly: Divergent Paths for American Dependents." *Demography* 21:435–57.

Pullam, T. W., 1982. "The Eventual Frequencies of Kin in a Stable Population." *Demography* 19:549–65.

Riley, M. W., 1983. "The Family in an Aging Society: A Matrix of Latent Relationships." *Journal of Family Issues* 4: 439–54.

Scharlach, A. E. and Boyd, S. L., 1989. "Caregiving and Employment: Results of an Employee Survey. *Gerontologist* 29:382–87.

Shanas, E., 1979. "Social Myth as Hypothesis: The Case of the Family Relations of Old People." *Gerontologist* 19:3–9.

Soldo, B. J., Wolf, D. and Agree, E. M., 1990. "Family, Households, and Care Arrangements of Frail Older Women: A Structural Analysis." *Journal of Gerontology* 45:238–49.

Stephens, S. and Christianson, J., 1986. *Informal Care of the Elderly*. Lexington, Mass.: D. C. Heath.

Stone, R. I. and Kemper, P., 1989. "Spouses and Children of Disabled Elders: How Large a Constituency for Long-Term Reform?" *Milbank Quarterly* 67:485–506.

Stone, R. I., Cafferata, G. L. and Sangl, J., 1987. "Caregivers of the Frail Elderly: A National Profile." *Gerontologist* 27:616–26.

Verbrugge, L. M., 1984. "Longer Life but Worsening Health? Trends in Health and Mortality of Middle-Aged and Older Persons." *Milbank Quarterly* 62:475–519.

Watkins, S. C., Menken, J. A. and Bongaarts, J., 1987. "Demographic Foundations of Family Change." *American Sociological Review* 52:346–58.

Chapter 17

On Lok: The Family Continuum

Doreen Der-McLeod and Jennie Chin Hansen

On Lok Senior Health Services of San Francisco, a nationally recognized innovator in long-term care, enables frail elderly persons who are certified for nursing home care to remain in their community for as long as possible. On Lok combines primary medical, adult day health, and homecare services—complete with transportation. Although the designated client (called "participant" at On Lok) is the elderly individual, in reality On Lok provides not only eldercare but family care, because care at On Lok is usually given "until death do us part." Most participants leave On Lok only at death, after four or more years in the program.

Working with families is integral to caring for On Lok's diverse elders, and On Lok employs diverse approaches tailored to each family's particular life situation and ethnicity. Participants range in age from 58 to 105. Many of the family caregivers are themselves elderly (50–80 years old), but sometimes a grandchild, a niece, or a nephew is the primary care-provider. On Lok's participant population is multiethnic: Chinese, Italian, Spanish, African American, German, Greek, Irish, Filipino, and Korean. The Chinese participants, who make up 80 percent of current enrollees, are by no means a homogeneous group, as a result of acculturation and an immigration pattern that has spanned more than a hundred years. Family support varies, often inversely with the number of years lived in America.

On Lok staff begin collaborating with families at intake, supplementing their care and relieving some of the stress of care-providing. Family involvement is assessed to ascertain the amount of support or burnout by various family members. To delineate the family members' respective roles, their relationship to the elder, and family dynamics in providing care, On Lok uses a family diagram as part of the assessment tool. The interdisciplinary team meets with the elder and family to share the assessment findings.

Through the assessment process, family care-providers acquire new knowledge and management skills and increase their ability to cope with the difficulties of providing care for a family member, whether he or she is suffering from Alzheimer's disease or another chronic illness (diabetes, cardiovascular disease, or Parkinson's, for example) that causes gradual but progressive loss of functioning (Keizer and Feins, 1991). Information provided by On Lok's team about the elder's health status, including cognitive and functioning abilities and deficits, helps the family to understand and share their concerns about providing care. For example, the family of a demented elder often does not know that the dementia is a disease or illness and attributes loss of memory or confusion to normal aging. However, the team also recognizes that denial helps some families cope with the pain of the relative's dementia (Cohen and Eisdorfer, 1986; Powell and Courtice, 1983).

In addition to helping families cope with chronic, progressive illness, On Lok helps them recognize changes, such as decrease in appetite or further loss of cognition, that can signal further decline for the elder. The team works with the family to reorganize the care plan to meet changing needs. Basic social work interventions help a family member reorganize and adjust to chronic illness, and ultimately to the placement or death of the elder. In addition to educating family members about illness and recommending reading materials, these interventions include listening, validating feelings, providing affirmation to care-providers, and ongoing evaluation of the participant and the family situation.

On Lok also helps the family by helping the participant articulate how much intervention is desired in the event of a health crisis. Given the frailty of On Lok's population, a health crisis is inevitable for virtually every participant. In the last six years, On Lok has developed a policy of soliciting health wishes from participants. Establishing health wishes is a *process* at On Lok—a dialogue between the healthcare provider, the participant, and the family. This process recognizes the individual's right to make autonomous healthcare decisions while acknowledging that decisions are rarely developed in isolation; in the real world, there is heavy reliance on family members (Collopy, 1988).

Six months after enrollment, when a trusting relationship with On Lok staff has developed, the participant's primary physician and a nurse or social worker initiate a discussion with the participant (if competent) about health wishes. The participant is informed that this information will guide the medical team in providing the care desired. Issues of cardiac pulmonary resuscitation or naso-gastric tube feeding are discussed. Given the unspoken tradition among Chinese and Italians of not discussing matters of death or dying, many participants have been surprisingly clear about their code status. When asked whether they want CPR to be administered if their heart should stop suddenly, many have been very direct: "I have lived a long time. Do not pound on my chest. Let me go peacefully." An 88-year-old woman answered this question more euphemistically: "I have traveled a long road." When asked, "How much further would you like this road to be?" she responded, "The road is long enough." The decision about the long-term use of a naso-gastric tube for feeding is more difficult—many say they want to make that decision later.

Some elders simply do not want to discuss these issues. They will say that they do not want to talk about it or refer the team to their oldest son or another family member. When a participant chooses to share the burden of healthcare decision-making with a family member, the physician and the nurse or social worker meet with the pertinent family member. As stated by Kapp (1991), "Shared decision making in a timely manner affords an opportunity for ongoing dialogue that informs future surrogates more fully about the patient's values and preferences regarding future decision making. Thus, sharing authority today is one way for a person to help fulfill the moral responsibility to plan for tomorrow." When a participant neither wants to discuss health wishes nor requests that this discussion be held instead with a family member, On Lok staff ask the participant more general questions in order to better understand what "quality of life" means for that participant. For example, "What do you still hope to see or do (e.g., see the birth of a great-grandchild)? What do you enjoy in life? What do you not enjoy?"

In conclusion, On Lok cares for an older person as a member of a family system. Although family needs are diverse, unique, and changing, they are still somewhat predictable. On Lok's approach helps prepare each family to survive the chronic disease process experienced by their relative, including crises of life and death, as positively as possible.

*   *   *

Doreen Der-McLeod, M.S.W., L.C.S.W., is social work supervisor, and Jennie Chin Hansen, R.N., M.S., is director, On Lock Senior Health Services, San Francisco.

REFERENCES

Cohen, D. and Eisdorfer, C., 1986. *The Loss of Life.* New York: W. W. Norton.

Collopy, B., 1988. "Autonomy in Long Term Care: Some Crucial Distinctions." *Gerontologist* 28 (Suppl.):10–17.

Kapp, M. B., 1991. "Health Care Decision Making by the Family: I Get By with a Little Help from My Family." *Gerontologist* 31(5):619–23.

Keizer, J. and Feins, L., 1991. "Intervention Strategies to Use in Counseling Families of Demented Patients." *Journal of Gerontological Social Work* 17(1/2): 201–16.

Powell, L. S. and Courtice, K., 1983. *Alzheimer's Disease, A Guide for Families.* Reading, Mass.: Addison-Wesley.

Chapter 18

Resources: Families and Aging

Ute J. Bayen

Not all important topics pertinent to the older person and the family could be covered in the chapters of this volume. We therefore provide a complementary list of resources that can guide further readings in this area.

JOURNALS TO WATCH

Articles pertinent to the aging family are published in journals of aging as well as journals of family studies. The following gerontological journals occasionally publish articles about the older adult and the family:

Generations, The Gerontologist, International Journal of Aging and Human Development, Journal of Aging and Social Policy, Journal of Aging Studies, Journal of Applied Gerontology, Journal of Cross-Cultural Gerontology, Journal of Gerontological Social Work, Journal of Gerontology, Journal of Women and Aging, Psychology and Aging, and *Research on Aging.*

Articles dealing with the aging family can also be found in the following journals dedicated to family issues:

Families in Society, Family Relations, Family Therapy, Journal of Family Issues, and *Journal of Marriage and the Family.*

BOOKS AND MONOGRAPHS

In recent years, a number of recommendable books addressing issues pertinent to the late-life family have been published for researchers and practitioners as well as for family members of elderly persons.

Allen, K. R., 1989. *Single Women/Family Ties: New Perspectives on Family*. Newbury Park, Calif.: Sage Publications.

This book focuses on the small percentage of women who never get married and compares them to married mothers. Interviews with 15 lifelong single women and 15 widows born in 1910 reveal life course patterns characterized by family-keeping roles in both groups. Never-married women held important roles such as parent caregiver, lifelong companion, aunt, and surrogate mother. Widows held the family positions of wife, mother, grandmother, and great-grandmother. Thus both groups find themselves in family-keeping roles as part of the traditional female caregiving career.

Brubaker, T. H., ed., 1990. *Family Relationships in Later Life*, 2d ed. Newbury Park, Calif.: Sage Publications.

This book provides a review of the research on family relationships (marriage, parent–adult child relations, siblings, and grandparents) and on social issues related to the later-life family (e.g., retirement, sexuality and gender roles, widowhood, divorce, abuse, minority issues). It also focuses on practice and policy aspects.

Bumagin, V. E. and Hirn, K. F., 1979. *Aging Is a Family Affair*. New York: Crowell.

This book addresses family members of all generations. Using case histories and anecdotes, it examines a broad range of issues pertinent to families of older persons. Topics are social changes, economics of aging, physical changes, enjoying the generation gap, and death in the family.

Carlin, V. F., 1987. *Where Can Mom Live? A Family Guide to Living Arrangements for Elderly Parents*. Lexington, Mass.: Lexington Books.

Based on the experiences of real families, this book describes alternative housing options for elderly parents, for example, home or apartment sharing, group homes, and congregate and lifecare communities. It examines psychological, social, and practical aspects of these living arrangements.

Connidis, I. A., 1989. *Family Ties and Aging. Perspectives on Individual and Population Aging.* Toronto: Butterworth.

This Canadian study analyzes four dimensions of family structure and family ties in later years, namely, the availability of kin, the amount of contact and type of interaction with kin, the nature of support or exchange relationships, and the quality of family relationships.

Gibson, D. and Gibson, R., 1991. *The Sandwich Years: When Your Kids Need Friends and Your Parents Need Parenting.* Grand Rapids, Mich.: Baker Book House.

This guidebook is written for members of the so-called "sandwich generation" who find themselves between the needs of their children on the one hand and those of their aging parents on the other. The book is designed to promote reconciliation and understanding between generations.

Hughston, G. A., Christopherson, V. A. and Bonjean, M. J., eds., 1989. *Aging and Family Therapy, Practitioner Perspectives on Golden Pond.* New York: Haworth Press. Has also been published in *Journal of Psychotherapy & the Family*, 1988, 5(1/2).

This is a collection of articles that discuss the application of mostly systemic models and intervention strategies for specific problems dealt with by therapists working with aging families: caregiving, mental illness, depression, sexual dysfunction, alcohol misuse, retirement, and bereavement.

Mancini, J. A., ed., 1989. *Aging Parents and Adult Children.* Lexington, Mass.: Lexington Books.

This book addresses professionals who work with older families as well as researchers interested in the study of aging families. The four parts discuss family structure and kin context, parent-child dynamics and interaction, caregiving and care-receiving, and future perspectives on theory and research.

Rossi, A. S. and Rossi, P. H., 1990. *Of Human Bonding: Parent-Child Relations across the Life Course.* Social Institutions and Social Change. New York: Aldine de Gruyter.

This book offers a lifespan perspective on changes in different aspects of parent-child relationships, such as distribution of responsibility, mutual assistance, and time perspectives.

Steinmetz, S., 1988. *Duty Bound: Elder Abuse and Family Care*. New-bury Park, Calif.: Sage Publications.

This volume addresses researchers as well as practitioners and examines how the burdens of caregiving for an elderly family member can be related to neglect and abuse.

Troll, L. E., ed., 1986. *Family Issues in Current Gerontology*. New York: Springer.

This book provides reviews and original research articles on changes in marital relations over time, widowhood, parent-child relations, caregiving, living arrangements, kinship networks, and childlessness and divorce.

ARTICLES AND BOOK CHAPTERS

The following list contains some review articles as well as selected research articles that present timely issues related to the older adult and the family.

Review

Bengtson, V., Rosenthal, C. and Burton, L., 1990. "Families and Aging: Diversity and Heterogeneity." In R. H. Binstock and L. K. George, eds., *Handbook of Aging and the Social Sciences*, 3d ed. New York: Academic Press.

Blieszner, R., 1986. "Trends in Family Gerontology Research." *Family Relations* 35(4):555–62.

Brubaker, T. H., 1990. "Continuity and Change in Later Life Families: Grandparenthood, Couple Relationships and Family Caregiving." *Gerontology Review* 3(1):24–40.

Treas, J. and Bengtson, V., 1987. "The Family in Later Years." In M. B. Sussman and S. K. Steinmetz, eds., *Handbook of Marriage and the Family*. New York: Plenum Press.

Marital Relationship

Lauer, R. H., Lauer, J. C. and Kerr, S. T., 1990. "The Long-Term Marriage: Perceptions of Stability and Satisfaction." *International Journal of Aging and Human Development* 31(3):189–96.

Peterson, C. C., 1990. "Husbands' and Wives' Perceptions of Marital Fairness across the Family Life Cycle." *International Journal of Aging and Human Development* 31(3): 179–88.

Steitz, J. A. and Welker, K. G., 1990. "Remarriage in Later Life: A Critique and Review of the Literature." *Journal of Women and Aging* 2(4):81–90.

Aging Parents and Adult Children

Aldous, J., Klaus, E. and Klein, D. M., 1985. "The Understanding Heart: Aging Parents and Their Favorite Children." *Child Development* 56(2):303–16.

Barnett, R. C. et al., 1991. "Adult Daughter–Parent Relationships and Their Associations with Daughter's Subjective Well-Being and Psychological Distress." *Journal of Marriage and the Family* 53(1):29–42.

Bengtson, V. L. and Roberts, R. E. L., 1991. "Intergenerational Solidarity in Aging Families: An Example of Formal Theory Construction." *Journal of Marriage and the Family* 53(4):856–70.

Berman, H. J., 1987. "Adult Children and Their Parents: Irredeemable Obligation and Irreplaceable Loss." *Journal of Gerontological Social Work* 10(1/2):21–34.

Cooney, T. M., 1989. "Co-residence with Adult Children: A Comparison of Divorced and Widowed Women." *Gerontologist* 29(6):779–84.

Crimmins, E. M. and Ingegneri, D. G., 1990. "Interaction and Living Arrangements of Older Parents and Their Children: Past Trends, Present Determinants, Future Implications." *Research on Aging* 12(1):3–35.

Dewit, D. J., Wister, A. V. and Burch, T. K., 1988. "Physical Distance and Social Contact between Elders and Their Adult Children." *Research on Aging* 10(1):56–89.

Greenberg, J. R., 1991. "Problems in the Lives of Adult Children: Their Impact on Aging Parents." *Journal of Gerontological Social Work* 16(3/4): 149–61.

Hamon, R. R. and Blieszner, R., 1990. "Filial Responsibility Expectations among Adult Child–Older Parent Pairs." *Journals of Gerontology* 45(3):110–12.

Houser, B. B. and Berkman, S. L., 1984. "Aging Parent/Mature Child Relationships." *Journal of Marriage and the Family* 46(2):295–99.

Krout, J. A., 1988. "Rural versus Urban Differences in Elderly Parents' Contact with Their Children." *Gerontologist* 28(2):198–203.

Mancini, J. A. and Blieszner, R., 1989. "Aging Parents and Adult Children: Research Themes in Intergenerational Relations." *Journal of Marriage and the Family* 51(2):275–90.

Mercier, J. M., Paulson, L. and Morris, E. W., 1989. "Proximity as a Mediating Influence on the Perceived Aging Parent–Adult Child Relationship." *Gerontologist* 29(6):785–91.

Moss, M. S., Moss, S. Z. and Moles, E. L., 1985. "The Quality of Relationships between Elderly Parents and their Out-of-Town Children." *Gerontologist* 25(2)134–40.

Post, S. G., 1990. "Women and Elderly Parents: Moral Controversy in an Aging Society." *Hypatia: A Journal of Feminist Philosophy* 5(1):83–89.

Spitze, G. and Logan, J. R., 1989. "Gender Differences in Family Support: Is There a Payoff?" *Gerontologist* 29(1):108–13.

Spitze, G. and Logan, J. R., 1990. "Sons, Daughters, and Intergenerational Social Support." *Journal of Marriage and the Family* 52(2): 420–30.

Stueve, A. and O'Donnell, L., 1989. "Interactions between Women and their Elderly Parents: Constraints of Daughters' Employment." *Research on Aging* 11(3):331–53.

Suitor, J. J. and Pillemer, K., 1988. "Explaining Intergenerational Conflict When Adult Children and Elderly Parents Live Together." *Journal of Marriage and the Family* 50(4):1037–47.

Talbott, M. M., 1990. "The Negative Side of the Relationship between Older Widows and Their Adult Children: The Mothers' Perspective." *Gerontologist* 30(5): 595–603.

Uhlenberg, P. and Cooney, T. M., 1990. "Family Size and Mother-Child Relations in Later Life." *Gerontologist* 30(5):618–25.

Walker, A. J. and Thompson, L., 1983. "Intimacy and Intergenerational Aid and Contact among Mothers and Daughters." *Journal of Marriage and the Family* 45(4): 841–49.

Walker, A. J. and Pratt, C. C., 1991. "Daughters' Help to Mothers: Intergenerational Aid Versus Caregiving." *Journal of Marriage and the Family* 53(1):3–12.

MULTIGENERATIONAL LIVING ARRANGEMENTS

Aquilino, W. S. and Supple, K. R., 1991. "Parent–Adult Child Relations and Parent's Satisfaction with Living Arrangements When Adult Children Live at Home." *Journal of Marriage and the Family* 53(1):13–28.

Brackbill, Y. and Kitch, D., 1991. "Intergenerational Relationships: A Social Exchange Perspective on Joint Living Arrangements among the Elderly and Their Relatives." *Journal of Aging Studies* 5(1):77–97.

Chappell, N. L., 1991. "In-Group Differences among Elders Living with Friends and Family Other Than Spouses." *Journal of Aging Studies* 5(1):61–76.

Coward, R. T. and Cutler, S. J., 1991. "The Composition of Multi-generational Households That Include Elders." *Research on Aging* 13(1):55–73.

Coward, R. T., Cutler, S. J. and Schmidt, F. E., 1989. Differences in the Household Composition of Elders by Age, Gender, and Area of Residence. *Gerontologist* 29(6):814–21.

Mogey, J. et al., 1990. "The Aged in the United States: Kinship and Household." In J. Mogey, ed., *Aiding and Aging: The Coming Crisis in Support for the Elderly by Kin and State. Contributions to the Study of Aging, No. 17*. New York: Greenwood Press.

SOCIAL SUPPORT

Connidis, I. A. and Davies, L., 1990. "Confidants and Companions in Later Life: The Place of Family and Friends." *Journal of Gerontology: Social Sciences* 45(4):S141–49.

Johnson, C. L., 1983. "Dyadic Family Relations and Social Support." *Gerontologist* 23(4):377–83.

Johnson, C. L., 1992. "Family Functioning in Late Late Life." *Journal of Gerontology: Social Sciences* 47(2):S66–S72.

McCulloch, B. J., 1990. "The Relationship of Intergenerational Reciprocity of Aid to the Morale of Older Parents: Equity and Exchange

Theory Comparisons." *Journal of Gerontology: Social Sciences* 45(4): S150–55.

Morgan, D. L., Schuster, T. L. and Butler, E. W., 1991. "Role Reversals in the Exchange of Social Support." *Journal of Gerontology: Social Sciences* 46(5):S278–87.

Wellman, B. and Wortley, N. S., 1990. "Brothers' Keepers: Situating Kinship Relations in Broader Networks of Social Support." In J. Mogey, ed., *Aiding and Aging: The Coming Crisis in Support for the Elderly by Kin and State. Contributions to the Study of Aging, No. 17.* New York: Greenwood Press.

INTERVENTION

Duffy, M., 1984. "Aging and the Family: Intergenerational Psychodynamics." *Psychotherapy* 21(3):342–46.

Genevay, B., 1990. "The Aging-Family Consultation. A 'Summit Conference' Model of Brief Therapy." *Generations* 14(1):58–60.

Greene, R., 1989. "A Life Systems Approach to Understanding Parent-Child Relationships in Aging Families." *Journal of Psychotherapy and the Family* 5(1/2):57–69.

Ingersoll-Dayton, B. and Arndt, B., 1990. "Uses of the Genogram with the Elderly and Their Families." *Journal of Gerontological Social Work* 15(1/2):105–20.

Mathis, R. D. and Tanner, Z., 1991. "Cohesion, Adaptability, and Satisfaction of Family Systems in Later Life." *Family Therapy* 18(1):47–60.

Patten, P. C. and Piercy, F. P., 1989. "Dysfunctional Isolation in the Elderly: Increasing Marital and Family Closeness Through Improved Communication." *Contemporary Family Therapy. An International Journal* 11(2):131–47.

OTHER AREAS OF INTEREST

Aldous, J., 1987. New Views on the Family Life of the Elderly and the Near-Elderly. *Journal of Marriage and the Family* 49(2):227–34.

Allen, K. R., 1989. "Continuities and Discontinuities in Elderly Women's Lives: An Analysis of Four Family Careers." In D. Unruh and G. S. Livings, eds., *Personal History through the Life Course. Current*

Perspectives on Aging and the Life Cycle: A Research Annual, vol.3. Greenwich, Conn.: JAI Press.

Hays, J. A., 1984. "Aging and Family Resources: Availability and Proximity of Kin." *Gerontologist* 24(2):149–53.

High, D. M., 1991. "A New Myth about Families of Older People?" *Gerontologist* 31(5):611–18.

Lehr, U. and Kruse, A., 1990. "The Multigenerational Family—Theoretical and Empirical Contributions." In M. Bergener and S. I. Finkel, eds., *Clinical and Scientific Psychogeriatrics, Vol. 1, The Holistic Approaches*. New York: Springer.

Mullins, L. C., Johnson, D. P. and Andersson, L., 1987. "Loneliness of the Elderly: The Impact of Family and Friends." *Special Issue: Loneliness: Theory, Research and Applications, Journal of Social Behavior and Personality* 2(2):225–38.

Peterson, C. C. and Peterson, J. L., 1988. "Older Men's and Women's Relationships with Adult Kin: How Equitable Are They?" *International Journal of Aging and Human Development* 27(3):221–31.

Stephens, M. A. P. and Hobfoll, S. E., 1990. Ecological Perspectives on Stress and Coping in Later-Life Families. In M. A. P. Stephens et al., eds., *Stress and Coping in Later-Life Families. Series in Applied Psychology: Social Issues and Questions*. New York: Hemisphere.

*   *   *

Ute J. Bayen, M.S., is a doctoral candidate in the Department of Human Development and Family Studies, The Pennsylvania State University.